R.H. BOYD

EST. 1896

Vol. 129 • No. 1

AF207605

Our Mission: R.H. Boyd empowers our community by providing educational, inspirational, and culturally relevant content, services, and events.

Our Vision: Our vision is to impact tomorrow through influential storytelling, culturally relevant educational content, scholarship and grant support, and transformative leadership training. We are dedicated to uplifting our community, amplifying diverse voices, and fostering a legacy of excellence in publishing, multimedia resources, and events.

Our Motto: Teach. Lead. Inspire.

R. H. BOYD, DD, LLD
Founder (1896–1922)

H. A. BOYD, DD
(1922–1959)

T. B. BOYD, JR., DD
(1959–1979)

T. B. BOYD III, DD
(1979–2017)

LaDonna Boyd, EdD
President/CEO

Emmanuel J. LeGrair, M.Ed.
Creative Director

Keaton Bell, BBA
Director of Finance

Steven Puckett, AAS
Director of Operations

EDITORIAL STAFF:

Olivia M. Cloud, MRE
(Associate Editor)

Monique Gooch, BA
Sinclaire Sparkman, MABTS
Brittany Batson, BA
Carla Davis, BA

Writer:
Christina Zimmerman

Follow us for the latest news and updates!

   @rhboydco

Adult Christian LIFE

Adult Christian Life contains Sunday school material for mature believers. The exposition of the Scripture, with life-centered insights, is preceded by an introduction to the lesson designed to help learners gain a greater understanding of the text under discussion relative to context, content, and meaning of life.

Lesson material is based on the International Uniform Sunday School Lesson Outlines, copyrighted by the Division of Christian Education, the National Council of the Churches of Christ in the U.S.A., and is used with permission.

Scriptures taken from the *New Revised Standard Version Updated Edition* of the Bible, © 2022 by the Division of Christian Education of the National Council of Churches of Christ in the United States of America. Used by permission. All rights reserved.

Adult Christian Life (USPS 006-480) (ISSN 1947-6604), copyright © 2025 by R.H. Boyd Company, 6717 Centennial Blvd., Nashville, Tennessee 37209-1017. *Adult Christian Life* is published quarterly by R.H. Boyd Company. Periodicals postage paid at Nashville, Tennessee.

POSTMASTER: Send address changes to *Adult Christian Life*, R.H. Boyd Company, 6717 Centennial Blvd., Nashville, Tennessee 37209-1017.

For Customer Service 24 hours a day, call 1-877-4RHBOYD.

@rhboydco

INSIDE
ADULT CHRISTIAN LIFE

The *Adult Christian Life* quarterly has many
features that appeal to adult students.

Printed Scripture Passage: The *King James Version* and the *NRSVue* are listed side by side so learners can compare traditional and contemporary translations of God's Word. The main thought verse is highlighted in bold text.

Suggested Opening Exercises: This feature, standard to all R.H. Boyd Sunday school quarterlies, remains popular among learners and leaders alike.

Quarterly Overview: This gives a general description of the lessons to be studied during the quarter.

Know It: Contextualizes the lesson and expands on its truths to stimulate additional questions, interest, or action on the part of the learners.

Remember It: Summary section that emphasizes the most relevant points of the lesson and highlights how the lesson applies to learners.

Hear It: An opportunity to listen to the relevant message of the lesson through music.

Live It: Suggestions for learners to take specific action to make the lesson a personal opportunity for spiritual enlightenment.

Share It: Suggestions for learners to spread the Bible truth learned through various mediums, such as social media or one-on-one talks.

Daily Devotional Readings: Daily Bible readings to prepare learners for the Sunday lesson experience.

Online Extras: Activities, quizzes, and additional resources for outside study via *www.rhboyd.com.*

Contents: April, May, June

SUGGESTED OPENING EXERCISES

1. Usual Signal for Beginning

2. Prayer (Closing with the Lord's Prayer)

3. Singing (Songs to Be Selected)

4. Scripture Reading: 1 Peter 4:8–11 (KJV)

Director: And above all things have fervent charity among yourselves: for charity shall cover the multitude of sins.

School: Use hospitality one to another without grudging.

Director: As every man hath received the gift, even so minister the same one to another, as good stewards of the manifold grace of God.

All: If any man speak, let him speak as the oracles of God; if any man minister, let him do it as of the ability which God giveth: that God in all things may be glorified through Jesus Christ, to whom be praise and dominion for ever and ever. Amen.

Recitation in Concert:

Ephesians 4:2–3 (KJV)

2 With all lowliness and meekness, with longsuffering, forbearing one another in love;

3 Endeavouring to keep the unity of the Spirit in the bond of peace.

CLOSING WORK

1. Singing

2. Sentences: Revelation 5:11–12

11 And I beheld, and I heard the voice of many angels round about the throne and the beasts and the elders: and the number of them was ten thousand times ten thousand, and thousands of thousands;

12 Saying with a loud voice, Worthy is the Lamb that was slain to receive power, and riches, and wisdom, and strength, and honour, and glory, and blessing.

Dismissal with Prayer

   @rhboydco

IT ONLY TAKES ONE

BACKGROUND PASSAGE: HEBREWS 9:23–10:25
PRINT PASSAGE: HEBREWS 9:23–28, 10:2–4, 11–14, 19–22

RESOURCES: *New National Baptist Hymnal 21st Century Edition,*
Boyd's Commentary for the Sunday School

KEY VERSE: For Christ is not entered into the holy places made with hands, which are the figures of the true; but into heaven itself, now to appear in the presence of God for us: (Hebrews 9:24, KJV)

Intro

Many pet owners will do whatever it takes to protect their pets from dangerous situations. Dogs, cats, and other pets are often regarded as members of their human families and, as such, are loved and protected from harm. So, pet lovers will understand a dog owner's sacrificial efforts to protect her beloved canines when a fox wanders into the yard. This happened recently in suburban Atlanta. Despite the possibility of being bitten by a rabid fox, a dog owner stepped forward and did all she could to chase the fox away. Rather than run to save herself, she acted sacrificially to save her two dogs.

The word "sacrifice" applies to selfless acts made on behalf of others. Today's culture understands the meaning of sacrifice because, at some point in life, each of us has been either the recipient of a sacrifice or made one for the sake of another. Consider the sacrifices parents make for the wellbeing of their children.

The ultimate sacrifice, however, is the giving one's life on behalf of others. Dr. Martin Luther King, Jr., whose assassination we commemorated two days ago, refused to give up the fight for freedom and equality even though it cost his life.

The devastating wildfires in greater Los Angeles put the lives of thousands of first responders at risk. Nevertheless, firefighters from across the country, and even some from other nations voluntarily came to help with the disaster. We celebrate Memorial Day to remember the military personnel who gave their lives for our country. Yet there is one sacrifice that surpasses all others—the sacrifice of Jesus Christ. He stood between humanity and sin and gave His life for the world. Because of this, no one has to experience the wrath of God.

Think About It

In what ways has being a believer helped you understand the nature of sacrifice? How can we help others understand how sacrifice relates to Christian salvation?

_____

_____

_____

1. The Old Way (Hebrews 9:23–28, 10:2–4)

King James Version	NRSVue
IT was therefore necessary that the patterns of things in the heavens should be purified with these; but the heavenly things themselves with better sacrifices than these.	THUS it was necessary for the sketches of the heavenly things to be purified with these rites, but the heavenly things themselves need better sacrifices than these.
24 For Christ is not entered into the holy places made with hands, which are the figures of the true; but into heaven itself, now to appear in the presence of God for us:	**24** For Christ did not enter a sanctuary made by human hands, a mere copy of the true one, but he entered into heaven itself, now to appear in the presence of God on our behalf.
25 Nor yet that he should offer himself often, as the high priest entereth into the holy place every year with blood of others;	**25** Nor was it to offer himself again and again, as the high priest enters the Holy Place year after year with blood that is not his own;
26 For then must he often have suffered since the foundation of the world: but now once in the end of the world hath he appeared to put away sin by the sacrifice of himself.	**26** for then he would have had to suffer again and again since the foundation of the world. But as it is, he has appeared once for all at the end of the age to remove sin by the sacrifice of himself.
27 And as it is appointed unto men once to die, but after this the judgment:	**27** And just as it is appointed for mortals to die once, and after that the judgment,
28 So Christ was once offered to bear the sins of many; and unto them that look for him shall he appear the second time without sin unto salvation.	**28** so Christ, having been offered once to bear the sins of many, will appear a second time, not to deal with sin, but to save those who are eagerly waiting for him.
• • • 10:2–4 • • •	• • • 10:2–4 • • • •
2 For then would they not have ceased to be offered? because that the worshippers once purged should have had no more conscience of sins.	**2** Otherwise, would they not have ceased being offered, since the worshipers, cleansed once for all, would no longer have any consciousness of sin?
3 But in those sacrifices there is a remembrance again made of sins every year.	**3** But in these sacrifices there is a reminder of sin year after year.
4 For it is not possible that the blood of bulls and of goats should take away sins.	**4** For it is impossible for the blood of bulls and goats to take away sins.

When we speak of "God's attributes," we speak of characteristics held only by the one, true God. One of these attributes is God's holiness. Scripture calls us to practice holiness (Lev. 11:44, 45; 19:2; 1 Peter 1:15–17). But God's holiness is beyond practice; it is perfected. God's holiness prevents Him from drawing near to sinful people. This does not mean that God does not love humanity—the people He created and with whom He desires communion. God doesn't draw near because He is utterly untainted and stands in awesome perfection and purity. He is a holy God who is set apart from sinful humanity.

This relationship gap was not the will of God, nor was it descriptive of a triune God. One of the reasons God created people to live in this world was so that humans could walk in full fellowship with their God. But the world God created changed when sin entered it. The original way was swallowed by a new way that wasn't necessarily the *right* way.

In other words, when sin entered, it became necessary to atone for the sins of God's people. To "atone" means to make amends for or make better. A sacrifice had to be made. Humanly speaking, because of the gravity of humanity's sin, a single sacrifice would not suffice. Sin is perpetual. This means that, over and over again, an animal had to be sacrificed to atone for the sins of the people so they could be forgiven.

The Israelite community understood that the forgiveness of sins demanded the shedding of blood (see e.g. Lev. 17:11). Their sins would be atoned for through the death of an animal and the outpouring of its blood on the altar. But, with Jesus' sacrifice, that way became the *old* way. Animal sacrifices were never able to fully atone, or take away, sin—thus the need for repeated animal sacrifices. They were only a foreshadow of Christ. Jesus is a perfect sacrifice, and only a perfect God–man could take away humanity's sin. The psalmist whose disobedience separated him from God recognized something else essential about sacrifices. Centuries before Christ, the psalmist said, "The sacrifice acceptable to God is a broken spirit; a broken and contrite heart, O God, you will not despise" (Ps. 51:17, NRSVue). God accepted the perfect sacrifice of Christ because Jesus' broken body represented submission to God's will.

The book of Hebrews explains how Christ offered a better sacrifice. After His death at Calvary, Christ entered heaven where God was located. The heavenly environment where Christ dwells is real and eternal, but the earthly Tabernacle was only a facsimile of that reality. The high priest entered this Tabernacle every year to offer animal sacrifices that had no choice in the matter. They were slain involuntarily. In contrast, Christ died only one time in history to atone for the sins of people throughout the course of time. Further, His death was voluntary. Christ's sacrifice was superior. He is alive and continually represents us before God. He prays for us, and He accomplishes what no one-time sacrifice could do. In a single act, Jesus fulfilled the old way and created a new way.

2. The New Way (Hebrews 10:11–14)

King James Version	NRSVue
11 And every priest standeth daily ministering and offering oftentimes the same sacrifices, which can never take away sins:	**11** And every priest stands day after day at his service, offering again and again the same sacrifices that can never take away sins.
12 But this man, after he had offered one sacrifice for sins for ever, sat down on the right hand of God;	**12** But when Christ had offered for all time a single sacrifice for sins, "he sat down at the right hand of God,"
13 From henceforth expecting till his enemies be made his footstool.	**13** and since then has been waiting "until his enemies would be made a footstool for his feet."
14 For by one offering he hath perfected for ever them that are sanctified.	**14** For by a single offering he has perfected for all time those who are sanctified.

Christ's sacrifice was effective because it lasted. The high priests endlessly offered sacrifices. There were daily and yearly sacrifices. Sacrifices were offered annually at the Day of Atonement and officiated by priests daily. The futility of the whole process is evident in verse 11: "And every priest stands day after day at his service, offering again and again the same sacrifices that can never take away sins" (NRSVue). Their standing was that their work was never done. But in verse 12, we learn that Christ sat down because His work on the cross was done. Sitting was a position of accomplishment. Jesus made the payment for the price of sin once and for all. Jesus was the sacrificial lamb. When He declared, "It is finished" (John 19:30), He meant it. Now Christ is in His exalted position at the right hand of God.

Through prayer Jesus provides unlimited access to the grace and power of God. There is another victory to come, and Christ is waiting for it. There will be a time when He will have victory over His enemies as stated in verse 13. The resurrection of Christ from the dead means He has already been victorious. But there will come a time when the spiritual enemies of Christ will be displayed in their position of defeat, as Jesus' footstool. Along with Christ, we also wait for this period. Until then, we must do the work of evangelists and share the message of Christ as led by God's Spirit at work in us.

One day Christ will enjoy full victory over His enemies. Seated on His throne in heaven, Jesus will reign forever and make a final display of triumph over evil (1 Cor. 15:22–28). After His once and for all sacrifice on the cross, resurrection from the dead, and ascension to heaven, believers benefit from a *new* way. Though we are not yet home, the work of Christ seated on the right hand of God as our High Priest secures our salvation. What a glorious benefit!

3. The Right Way (Hebrews 10:19–22)

King James Version	NRSVue
19 Having therefore, brethren, boldness to enter into the holiest by the blood of Jesus,	**19** Therefore, my friends, since we have confidence to enter the sanctuary by the blood of Jesus,
20 By a new and living way, which he hath consecrated for us, through the veil, that is to say, his flesh;	**20** by the new and living way that he opened for us through the curtain (that is, through his flesh),
21 And having an high priest over the house of God;	**21** and since we have a great priest over the house of God,
22 Let us draw near with a true heart in full assurance of faith, having our hearts sprinkled from an evil conscience, and our bodies washed with pure water.	**22** let us approach with a true heart in full assurance of faith, with our hearts sprinkled clean from an evil conscience and our bodies washed with pure water.

In the Temple, the Holy Place was sealed by a curtain that allowed only the High Priest to enter. The High Priest could only enter this holy room, which symbolized the presence of God, once a year. That was the Day of Atonement when sacrifices were made for the sins of the people. But because Jesus' death removed the curtain, all believers may walk into God's presence at any time. God has made Himself accessible to humanity. In view of what Jesus has done, we can approach God confidently. This is a relationship that the Israelites did not have through the old sacrificial process. Now, not only the priesthood but all believers can come into God's presence.

Therefore, we should not approach God weakly or half-heartedly. We should approach God with the same power of the risen Christ. This is the *right* way. We can now approach God and receive the mercy and grace of our High Priest. This blessing brings us many privileges.

We are encouraged to draw near to God in personal devotion. According to verse 22, we are given four conditions for approaching God. First, we are to come with a sincere heart. This calls for genuine devotion rather than hypocrisy. Second, we are to come in full assurance of faith. This demands a bold confidence, to which we are given full access through Christ alone. Third, we are to have our hearts sprinkled…from a guilty conscience. This demands constant openness to God for confession of our sins. Lastly, we are to have our bodies washed with pure water. This may be a reference to baptism as an outward commitment to Christ or it might be symbolic as is the reference to hearts sprinkled with blood. If it is symbolic, hearts sprinkled from a guilty conscience represents our salvation and washed bodies points to a righteous lifestyle. In this new state of purity made possible by Jesus, believers can come boldly to God and claim His grace and mercy.

Remember It

The death, burial, and resurrection of Jesus Christ was a sacrificial event. It empowered those who follow Him to live the kind of life that He lived. It inspired all those who profess Christianity to consider a new way to not only view life but also a right way to live it. As Jesus walked close to God, we should walk close to God. As Jesus extended kindness and love to others, we should do the same. Through His sacrifice, "...perceive we the love of God, because he laid down his life for us: and we ought to lay down our lives for the brethren" (1 John 3:16, KJV). We should be mindful that because of the love Christ demonstrated on the cross, we can live in readiness to sacrificially help others as needed.

• • • • • • • • • • • • • • • • • • •

Hear It

Celebrate the sacrifice of Christ through a time of personal worship and devotion. Use a music app or a songbook to compile and sing songs that express gratefulness for what Jesus has done. Make a new playlist reflecting your gratefulness and share it with others.

Live It

Following the sacrificial death of Christ, He ascended to heaven, and is now seated at the right hand of God interceding for every believer. Just like Christ, we should make prayer an essential part of our daily routine, seeking to develop a healthy prayer life.

Share It

Don't hide what Christ has done not only for you but for the whole world. Honor Jesus' sacrifice for your life by sharing a personal story. Share how Jesus' sacrifice made a difference for your life.

Get Social
Start an online conversation about **#SACRIFICE**. Share your views and tag us @rhboydco and use #rhboydco.

@rhboydco

DDR

Devotional Readings for April 7–13, 2025

MONDAY	TUESDAY	WEDNESDAY	THURSDAY	FRIDAY	SATURDAY	SUNDAY
Our Sins Have Hidden God's Face	Healed by Christ's Wounds	The Promise of Eternal Life	God So Loved the World	Atonement through His Blood	Reconciled to God by Christ	Atonement through God's Son
Isaiah 59:1–8	1 Peter 2:19–25	John 3:1–15	John 3:16–21	Romans 3:19–31	Romans 5:1–15	1 John 2:1-6; 4:9–17

ALL YOU NEED IS LOVE

BACKGROUND PASSAGE: 1 JOHN 2:1–6; 4:7–21
PRINT PASSAGE: 1 JOHN 2:1–6; 4:9–17

RESOURCES: *New National Baptist Hymnal 21st Century Edition,*
Boyd's Commentary for the Sunday School

KEY VERSE: In this is love, not that we loved God but that he loved us and sent his Son to be the atoning sacrifice for our sins. (1 John 4:10, NRSVue)

Intro

The phrase "fake news" has become popularized over the last decade. Many people believe that the phrase originated in recent political campaigns, when candidates weaponized lies to promote themselves. However, fake news, disinformation, hoaxes, and propaganda all mean the same and have been used throughout history. The goal of fake news is to damage the reputation of others or make money through false advertisement. At its roots, fake news is deception and the denial of truth. It is the weaponization of words in its deepest sense.

Today's social media has caused a rapid increase of fake news. Some people intentionally run a platform that promotes lies and conspiracy theories, such as "Infowars" founder Alex Jones. With fake news, Jones caused harm to many of the victims' families of the Sandy Hook massacre. His claim was that the massacre was a hoax. The lives of these families were put in danger by people who believed Jones. But through the legal efforts of the victims' families, Jones was held liable for creating fake news and was ordered to pay over one billion dollars in damages. That was a big price to pay for using the gift of words to tell a lie.

There are no lies in the Word of God. It is characterized by biblical scholars as the inerrant Word of God. This means that the Bible and every word in it is utterly true. When we read, "God loves the world" (John 3:16), we can believe beyond a shadow of a doubt that God's love is real. We can hold as complete truth that the acts, such as the work of Christ on the cross, are real acts of love.

Think About It

Sometimes truth is challenging to reconcile with "reality." How do you reconcile the truth that God loves the whole world with the calamities and chaos in the lives of individuals and whole countries?

_____

_____

_____

1. God's Love as a Solution for Sin (1 John 2:1–6)

King James Version	NRSVue
MY little children, these things write I unto you, that ye sin not. And if any man sin, we have an advocate with the Father, Jesus Christ the righteous:	MY little children, I am writing these things to you so that you may not sin. But if anyone does sin, we have an advocate with the Father, Jesus Christ the righteous;
2 And he is the propitiation for our sins: and not for ours only, but also for the sins of the whole world.	2 and he is the atoning sacrifice for our sins, and not for ours only but also for the sins of the whole world.
3 And hereby we do know that we know him, if we keep his commandments.	3 Now by this we may be sure that we know him, if we obey his commandments.
4 He that saith, I know him, and keepeth not his commandments, is a liar, and the truth is not in him.	4 Whoever says, "I have come to know him," but does not obey his commandments, is a liar, and in such a person the truth does not exist;
5 But whoso keepeth his word, in him verily is the love of God perfected: hereby know we that we are in him.	5 but whoever obeys his word, truly in this person the love of God has reached perfection. By this we may be sure that we are in him:
6 He that saith he abideth in him ought himself also so to walk, even as he walked.	6 whoever says, "I abide in him," ought to walk just as he walked.

Know It

Jesus' beloved disciple, the Apostle John, wrote the book of 1 John while living in Ephesus. One of the reasons he wrote this book is to deter believers from heretics that were teaching false doctrine in the area (1 John 2:26). The false teachings of that time included Gnosticism, Docetism, Cerinthianism, and others. The influence of these false teachings was strong enough to cause some Christians to turn from the truths of God and live disobediently. The false teachings of today have the same impact on believers. Rather than trusting the Word of God or seeking to discover whether facts are true, some believers are persuaded to live contrary to God's truth.

This is the sinful living that John addressed in his letter. This sin and unbelief were the behavior of the Christians in Ephesus. Apparently, they were Christians in name only—

NOTES:

those who claimed to know God but made no effort to keep God's commands. Rather than believe God, they believed the teachings of Gnosticism which distorted the truth through mysticism. Even more so, these believers did not seem to understand that sin had created a wall between them and God.

Further, John shows in this letter that our faith cannot be separated from our obedience and love for God. John set Christians, especially false believers, straight with the statement: "And hereby we do know that we know him, if we keep his commandments" (v. 3, KJV). John took this truth to another level when he wrote another truth: if we know God but disobey him, we are liars (v. 4). This does not mean that we live perfectly without sin, as this is something we cannot do. Rather, these verses reveal that the way we act shows the authenticity of our faith.

Christ-followers cannot live perfectly sinless lives, and John reminds us in 1 John 1:8 that if we believe we are sinless, we are living deceived lives and hopelessly separated from God. This was John's understanding about sin. We must accept the truth that we are sinners, but also that we have a Savior who forgives and cleanses us from sin (1 John 1:9). This reveals that God loves us enough to provide a way for us to escape the penalty of sin.

2. The Evidence of God's Love (1 John 4:9–12)

King James Version	NRSVue
9 In this was manifested the love of God toward us, because that God sent his only begotten Son into the world, that we might live through him.	**9** God's love was revealed among us in this way: God sent his only Son into the world so that we might live through him.
10 Herein is love, not that we loved God, but that he loved us, and sent his Son to be the propitiation for our sins.	**10** In this is love, not that we loved God but that he loved us and sent his Son to be the atoning sacrifice for our sins.
11 Beloved, if God so loved us, we ought also to love one another.	**11** Beloved, since God loved us so much, we also ought to love one another.
12 No man hath seen God at any time. If we love one another, God dwelleth in us, and his love is perfected in us.	**12** No one has ever seen God; if we love one another, God lives in us, and his love is perfected in us.

John reassures us that knowing God has benefits. If we know God and what He requires, and if we live in obedience to His commends, then the love of God will be expressed in our relationships. With one another, we express love through presence, gifts, or by use of the three words, "I love you." But John helps us understand that God loves us at a deeper level. God sacrificed His Son to redeem us and save us from His wrath. We can now live our lives through the life of Christ, who shows us how to live abundantly and in power.

In verse 10, John tells us that God did not express His love because we loved Him. On the contrary, God loved us first. But why does God love sinful humanity? The short answer is God loves us because of who He is. It is God's nature to love. God's love should not be viewed through the way the world defines love. The love of God is self–sacrifice. It's an unconditional love that loves us no matter what. The sacrifice of Jesus on the cross set a standard for all of us. No, we need not die a sacrificial death for anyone. When we love, God is honored and glorified because He is revealed in our lives.

Even though John tells us that no one has ever seen God, John wants us to understand that loving others as God loves helps others to see what God is like (v. 12). Our invisible God actually lives in us through the Holy Spirit. As He dwells in us, so also does His love dwell in us. The world sees God's love as it is expressed through our lives. The power and presence of God's love is fulfilled as He reaches out to the world through us.

3. The Assurance of God's Love (1 John 4:13–17)

King James Version	NRSVue
13 Hereby know we that we dwell in him, and he in us, because he hath given us of his Spirit.	**13** By this we know that we abide in him and he in us, because he has given us of his Spirit.
14 And we have seen and do testify that the Father sent the Son to be the Saviour of the world.	**14** And we have seen and do testify that the Father has sent his Son as the Savior of the world.
15 Whosoever shall confess that Jesus is the Son of God, God dwelleth in him, and he in God.	**15** God abides in those who confess that Jesus is the Son of God, and they abide in God.
16 And we have known and believed the love that God hath to us. God is love; and he that dwelleth in love dwelleth in God, and God in him.	**16** So we have known and believe the love that God has for us. God is love, and those who abide in love abide in God, and God abides in them.
17 Herein is our love made perfect, that we may have boldness in the day of judgment: because as he is, so are we in this world.	**17** Love has been perfected among us in this: that we may have boldness on the day of judgment, because as he is, so are we in this world.

Verse 13 looks back to verse 12. Here, the question of how God's love is expressed and made complete through us is answered. The answer: The Holy Spirit does it. The love we have for one another is dependent upon the Spirit of God living in us. Our capacity for any level of love is through the work of the Spirit at work in us. This is the way God's love is implanted in us as well as the way we know we live in God. Next, John helps us understand how God uses us to reach others. Our lives *in* God are to be lived *for* God. This is so that others might be reached with the Gospel. No one has ever seen Jesus in the flesh. We do, however, see the manifestation of God's love and presence through our lives lived in God. By this, we see Jesus, and by God's Spirit, we display God to the world.

We must trust the truth of God's Word, as the Bible is clear on what we should believe. God sent His Son, Jesus, to the cross to pay for our transgressions so we do not have to suffer the wages of sin. John reminds us in verses 14–15 that the testimony of our salvation reveals more than what Jesus did. Yes, Jesus saved us from sin, but we should also talk about who He is; He is the Son of God. This goes against the message of many false teachers then and now, in contemporary culture. In Ephesus, they spread many false claims about Christ, including that He was not qualified to die on the cross for our sins.

Similar to Romans 10:9, John makes clear that anyone who confesses Christ by mouth and believes in their heart that God raised Him from the dead is a true Christian. This is another form of testimony that affirms the reality of Jesus "in the flesh." That is to say, confessing Christ is an affirmation of one's belief in the tangible presence of God's glory in the earth.

Verses 16–17 conclude this section by reaffirming the role love plays in our salvation. John emphasizes that God is love and that the persons who live in love live in God, and God in them. According to John, this is the test of true Christianity. Through our lives, others must experience this God of love. That's the reason God sent His Son to die for us.

This life that we live as followers of Christ should be lived in love. It is a life that gives us the confidence needed to face Christ on the day of judgment. Such confidence comes because we live in love toward God and one another. The person who does not live in love may live in fear of judgment. The one who fears, expects punishment; but the one who loves expects to receive love. The Christian who lives in love toward God has nothing to fear on the day of judgment.

Remember It

The clash over truth and lies plays itself out daily throughout our culture, and the line for how to discern between the two grows dimmer, especially on television and by way of social media outlets. Many times, believers stand on opposing sides even from one another. But John urged those who are believers to do two things: to obey Christ in all things and to love fellow Christians. We should love because of the love of God. When we love others, it proves that we have God. Moreover, as we continue to live in God's love, we should reject false teachings and the sinfulness of this world that corrupts truth. Ultimately, the Apostle John helps us to love the way that God loves.

• • • • • • • • • • • • • • • • • • •

Share It • Live It • Hear It

There are many songs on YouTube and other music platforms about loving God. Download a few and use them to minister to God about the love you have for Him. He's worth it!

We have significant privileges because of our life in Christ. For one, we have a love relationship with the almighty God because His love lives in our hearts. This love gives us a level of peace and joy that we cannot find anywhere else in the world. This is guaranteed!

Filled with God's love, we can bless and help others in ways that will be surprising to them as well as us. Take time to lean into God for the sake of leaning into expressing the love of God. This week, intentionally reach out to someone who needs help in your community.

Get Social
Start an online conversation about **#REALLOVE**.
Share your views and tag us @rhboydco and use #rhboydco.

@rhboydco

DDR

Devotional Readings for April 14–20, 2025

MONDAY	TUESDAY	WEDNESDAY	THURSDAY	FRIDAY	SATURDAY	SUNDAY
I Will Rise Again	Made Perfect through Suffering	The Provider	Servanthood, Suspicion, and a Sign	Darkness, Despair, and Death	Ransomed!	He Has Risen!
				Matthew		
Psalm 71:12–24	Hebrews 2:1–13	Genesis 22:1–14	Matthew 26:17–30	27:39–40, 45–54	Psalm 49:1–15	Matthew 28:1–10

THEY COULDN'T KEEP HIM DOWN

BACKGROUND PASSAGE: MATTHEW 27:24–28:10
PRINT PASSAGE: MATTHEW 27:39–40, 45–54; 28:1–10

RESOURCES: *New National Baptist Hymnal 21st Century Edition,*
Boyd's Commentary for the Sunday School

KEY VERSE: And as they went to tell his disciples, behold, Jesus met them, saying, All hail. And they came and held him by the feet, and worshipped him.
(Matthew 28:9, KJV)

Intro

On September 11, 2001, terrorists flew two airplanes directly into the twin towers of the World Trade Center, toppling them to the ground. This event has gone down in American history as one of our darkest days. When construction of the buildings was completed in 1973, they stood as the tallest buildings in the world. A total of seven buildings made up the World Trade Center complex, which was able to accommodate approximately 130,000 people. These buildings represented the hearts of New Yorkers as well as the total American population. Many industries had a presence within the Center, including global and economic businesses. Popular culture filmmakers used it as a site for movies many times over.

A new World Trade Center has been erected where the former buildings stood. Completed in 2013, it includes six skyscrapers and other buildings, including a museum that memorializes the more than 2,500 people killed at the site on 9/11. Though lives were lost, the destruction of the old World Trade Center and the rise of a new complex can serve as a metaphor for the death and resurrection of our Savior, Jesus Christ. Like the resurrection of the World Trade Center, the resurrection of Christ was a memorable event of hope. Both are identified as a way forward after what was meant to cause harm to the lives of many. While the resurrection of the World Trade Center testifies to the strength and resilience of people, the resurrection of our Lord and Savior forever stands as a witness to the immense power of our loving Heavenly Father.

Think About It

How has God's redemptive power helped you to emerge from destructive or devastating circumstances in your life? How did you "bounce back" because of God's mercy? _____

_____

_____

1. Jesus Mocked on the Cross (Matthew 27:39–40)

King James Version	NRSVue
AND they that passed by reviled him, wagging their heads, **40** And saying, Thou that destroyest the temple, and buildest it in three days, save thyself. If thou be the Son of God, come down from the cross.	THOSE who passed by derided him, shaking their heads **40** and saying, "You who would destroy the temple and build it in three days, save yourself! If you are the Son of God, come down from the cross."

Know It

Matthew, a once despised tax collector, experienced a life change when Jesus called him to be a disciple. He wrote the book of Matthew to his fellow Jews to testify about the life of Christ, intending to prove Jesus to be the anticipated Messiah. Through his writings, Matthew provides details about the life, ministry, death, and resurrection of Christ. In the last few chapters of his book, Matthew focuses on Jesus' final days on earth. He writes about the Last Supper, Jesus' prayer in Gethsemane, the betrayal of Judas, Peter's denial, the trials of Jesus, His final words on the cross, and His burial in a borrowed tomb.

When Jesus was arrested, He underwent extreme suffering and merciless abuse at the hands of captors. Even so, He remained obedient to God's call, submitting Himself to be hung on the cross. Many people came out to not only watch this spectacle but to taunt and mock Jesus. Those who mocked Him brought to life Psalm 22:6–8: "But I am a worm, and no man; a reproach of men, and despised of the people. All they that see me laugh me to scorn: they shoot out the lip, they shake the head, saying, He trusted on the Lord that he would deliver him: let him deliver him, seeing he delighted in him" (KJV). Being beaten as badly as Jesus was means He was unrecognizable not only as the Messiah but as the Jesus they had known during the course of His earthly ministry. Jesus, the One who walked among them and ministered to their needs, was insulted instead of honored. He experienced a multi-layered abuse. Most people would not be able to endure the repetition of such emotional, intellectual, and physical taunting. One after another, a tirade of devastating harmful words and gestures were launched at Jesus as the Son of God.

In verse 40, the people use Jesus' own words against Him. They challenge Jesus to come down from the cross. The people did not understand that He was fully capable of saving Himself. He could have come down from the cross and stopped everything instantly. Instead, Jesus exercised obedience, love, and utter control to remain on the cross. Coming down would have been a tragedy for the whole human race. There would have been no redemption and no atonement of our sins. Only the sovereign King of the universe could have kept Himself on the cross. Truly, He was the almighty Savior of the world.

2. Jesus Died on the Cross (Matthew 27:45–54)

King James Version	NRSVue
45 Now from the sixth hour there was darkness over all the land unto the ninth hour.	**45** From noon on, darkness came over the whole land until three in the afternoon.
46 And about the ninth hour Jesus cried with a loud voice, saying, Eli, Eli, lama sabachthani? that is to say, My God, my God, why hast thou forsaken me?	**46** And about three o'clock Jesus cried with a loud voice, "Eli, Eli, lema sabachthani?" that is, "My God, my God, why have you forsaken me?"
47 Some of them that stood there, when they heard that, said, This man calleth for Elias.	**47** When some of the bystanders heard it, they said, "This man is calling for Elijah."
48 And straightway one of them ran, and took a spunge, and filled it with vinegar, and put it on a reed, and gave him to drink.	**48** At once one of them ran and got a sponge, filled it with sour wine, put it on a stick, and gave it to him to drink.
49 The rest said, Let be, let us see whether Elias will come to save him.	**49** But the others said, "Wait, let us see whether Elijah will come to save him."
50 Jesus, when he had cried again with a loud voice, yielded up the ghost.	**50** Then Jesus cried again with a loud voice and breathed his last.
51 And, behold, the veil of the temple was rent in twain from the top to the bottom; and the earth did quake, and the rocks rent;	**51** At that moment the curtain of the temple was torn in two, from top to bottom. The earth shook, and the rocks were split.
52 And the graves were opened; and many bodies of the saints which slept arose,	**52** The tombs also were opened, and many bodies of the saints who had fallen asleep were raised.
53 And came out of the graves after his resurrection, and went into the holy city, and appeared unto many.	**53** After his resurrection they came out of the tombs and entered the holy city and appeared to many.
54 Now when the centurion, and they that were with him, watching Jesus, saw the earthquake, and those things that were done, they feared greatly, saying, Truly this was the Son of God.	**54** Now when the centurion and those with him, who were keeping watch over Jesus, saw the earthquake and what took place, they were terrified and said, "Truly this man was God's Son!

Matthew notes that Jesus hung on the cross suffering and gasping for breath for three hours, from the sixth hour until the ninth hour. This was roughly from 9:00 a.m. until noon. During that time, darkness covered the whole land. Then, at noon, Jesus endured His deepest hurt; He felt the Father had turned

His back on His own Son. This is something we will never have to endure. God said in His Word that He will never leave us (Deut. 31:8). Many people turn their backs on God when they reject His Son or when they follow other gods, but God will never turn His back on those who love and follow Him.

Matthew tells us of four events that took place when Jesus died. First, at the moment of Jesus' death, the thick curtain that hung in the Temple separating all of humanity from the presence of God was torn in two from top to bottom. This was an indication of invitation. The way had been cleared for sinful people to enter the company of the holy God. The second event was the earth shaking and rocks splitting. Imagine the devastation of a climatic event so violent that rocks fall apart. This certainly would not have been a sign the people could ignore. The third event rests in the realm of the impossible. Some of the tombs around Jerusalem were opened and the buried bodies of many holy people were raised to life. Finally, verse 53 indicates that Jesus was not the only resurrected body to enter the holy city and be seen by many.

Verse 54 shares that centurions stationed around Jesus saw these things and were afraid. The original Greek indicates they were "startled by strange sights." With that, the centurions confess Jesus as the Son of God. This was a faith-response to the single, all-powerful God and the work of Jesus on the cross.

3. Jesus Rose from the Grave (Matthew 28:1–10)

King James Version	NRSVue
1 In the end of the sabbath, as it began to dawn toward the first day of the week, came Mary Magdalene and the other Mary to see the sepulchre.	**1** After the sabbath, as the first day of the week was dawning, Mary Magdalene and the other Mary went to see the tomb.
2 And, behold, there was a great earthquake: for the angel of the Lord descended from heaven, and came and rolled back the stone from the door, and sat upon it.	**2** And suddenly there was a great earthquake; for an angel of the Lord, descending from heaven, came and rolled back the stone and sat on it.
3 His countenance was like lightning, and his raiment white as snow:	**3** His appearance was like lightning, and his clothing white as snow.
4 And for fear of him the keepers did shake, and became as dead men.	**4** For fear of him the guards shook and became like dead men.
5 And the angel answered and said unto the women, Fear not ye: for I know that ye seek Jesus, which was crucified.	**5** But the angel said to the women, "Do not be afraid; I know that you are looking for Jesus who was crucified.
6 He is not here: for he is risen, as he said. Come, see the place where the Lord lay.	**6** He is not here; for he has been raised, as he said. Come, see the place where he lay.

3. Jesus Rose from the Grave (Matthew 28:1–10, Cont'd)

King James Version	NRSVue
7 And go quickly, and tell his disciples that he is risen from the dead; and, behold, he goeth before you into Galilee; there shall ye see him: lo, I have told you.	**7** Then go quickly and tell his disciples, 'He has been raised from the dead, and indeed he is going ahead of you to Galilee; there you will see him.' This is my message for you."
8 And they departed quickly from the sepulchre with fear and great joy; and did run to bring his disciples word.	**8** So they left the tomb quickly with fear and great joy, and ran to tell his disciples.
9 And as they went to tell his disciples, behold, Jesus met them, saying, All hail. And they came and held him by the feet, and worshipped him.	**9** Suddenly Jesus met them and said, "Greetings!" And they came to him, took hold of his feet, and worshiped him.
10 Then said Jesus unto them, Be not afraid: go tell my brethren that they go into Galilee, and there shall they see me.	**10** Then Jesus said to them, "Do not be afraid; go and tell my brothers to go to Galilee; there they will see me."

Mary Magdalene and Mary, the mother of James and Joseph, are identified as the first visitors to Jesus' tomb (see Matt. 28:1; 27:56). They got up early on the third day following the death of Jesus and made their way there. Once again, there is an earthquake—this time caused by an angel descending from heaven and rolling back the stone covering Jesus' tomb. The angel sits on the stone. Similar to Moses' face when he descended from the mountain after spending time with God (see Exod. 34:29), the angel's magnificent appearance may have been a response to being in God's presence. The power and appearance of the angel at the tomb cause the Roman guards to become afraid and faint (v. 4).

When the women arrive, they are also terrified by the brilliant angel sitting on the stone. But the angel both calms the women and gives them a reason to rejoice: Jesus, who had been crucified, is no longer in the tomb; He is resurrected, just as He said would happen (vv. 5–6). Invited to see for themselves, their faith is strengthened, and they are ready to testify!

However, their mission is interrupted; suddenly, there stands Jesus. He greets them with a simple "hello." They must have experienced many different emotions at this time. Jesus, who was crucified, was now before them. Like the angel, Jesus calms them and gives instructions: tell the disciples to go to Galilee and wait for Me. Excitedly, the women go on their way. Not only had a heavenly visitor reported Jesus' resurrection and shown them proof, but the King Himself had appeared to them! Verses 1–10 serve as proof to the world that Jesus is alive. Every person will have to choose to accept or reject Jesus as Lord and Savior. We will all be held accountable to a living Lord and will one day stand before Him.

Remember It

The story about the death of Jesus includes several people. There were those who accused Him, those who mocked Him, those who caused physical harm to Him, those who stood by and watched, and those who guarded Him. These are the attitudes and actions of people who did not really care anything about Jesus or who He claimed to be. But when Jesus was resurrected, the story changed. The women who loved and followed Him responded in awe. They fell at His feet and worshiped Him, not wanting to let Him go. May we open our hearts to understand and receive all the blessings and benefits the resurrection of Christ provides. May our attitudes and actions align with truth.

● ● ● ● ● ● ● ● ● ● ● ● ● ● ● ● ●

Share It • Live It • Hear It

Identify songs or hymns that celebrate the resurrection of Jesus Christ, then spend time honoring Him. You can do this by, first, meditating on the lyrics and then vocally praising Jesus.

Because of the resurrection of Christ, we can live in spiritual power by following His example. Even though He was the Son of God, Jesus humbled Himself and became obedient to the point of death. Jesus is our example; therefore, we must live in humble obedience to all that God requires.

The resurrection of Christ gives all who believe in Him eternal life. This is a gift worth sharing—something we resist keeping to ourselves. Consider the alternative if we don't share what God has done. Those of us who refuse Jesus as Lord and don't have eternal life will live eternally separated from God.

Get Social
Start an online conversation about **#RESURRECTION**. Share your views and tag us @rhboydco and use #rhboydco.

@rhboydco

DDR

Devotional Readings for April 21–28, 2025

	MONDAY	TUESDAY	WEDNESDAY	THURSDAY	FRIDAY	SATURDAY	SUNDAY
	Here Is the Lamb of God!	The Lord Has Become My Salvation	Live and Not Die	Worthy Ransom	Celebrate God	Live in the Light	The Slaughtered, Conquering Lamb
	John 1:29–36	Psalm 118:1–14	Psalm 118:15–29	1 Peter 1:13–25	Psalm 99	Revelation 21:9–16, 21–27	Revelation 5:1–10

SING A NEW SONG

BACKGROUND PASSAGE: REVELATION 5   **PRINT PASSAGE: REVELATION 5:1–10**

RESOURCES: *New National Baptist Hymnal 21st Century Edition,*
Boyd's Commentary for the Sunday School

KEY VERSE: They sing a new song: "You are worthy to take the scroll and to open its seals, you were slaughtered and by your blood you ransomed for God saints from every tribe and language and people and nation." (Revelation 5:9, NRSVue)

Intro

Singing is defined as making musical sounds with our voices. Historically, no one knows who sang the first song or when it was sung. Songs seemed to have grown out of the various experiences of people. Many songs, such as "We Shall Overcome," originated from hardship. This song developed over time through the input of several people. But when Dr. Martin Luther King, Jr. first heard it, its haunting tune stuck with him. Soon it became the anthem of the Civil Rights Movement. Like many songs in the Black tradition, it became a way to communicate the emotions, sorrows, and hope of an oppressed people. This certainly describes the traditional hymns and spirituals that people of African descent sang during Slavery. Most were songs of hope for a better life.

Spirituals transcribed and expressed words of weary hearts, tearful eyes, and hopeful spirits. They became an essential element in enslaved Black culture, highlighting suffering, raising morale, and giving instructions for safe passage. Because the enslaved endured limited freedoms, including communicating to one another, spirituals became a way to deliver messages to one another and to the God whom they believed would deliver them. When Jesus comes to carry us home, there will be singing in heaven. The songs may not be familiar spirituals, gospel songs, or even hymns but everyone will sing. Followers of Christ will have a place in the throne room of God, where we will join with angels and others in praise to the One who bore our sins, our Lord and Savior Jesus Christ.

Think About It

Praising Jesus changes things. How can songs of praise and worship help when we are facing difficult challenges in our lives?

_____

_____

_____

_____

1. Seeking the Worthy One (Revelation 5:1–4)

King James Version	NRSVue
AND I saw in the right hand of him that sat on the throne a book written within and on the backside, sealed with seven seals.	THEN I saw in the right hand of the one seated on the throne a scroll written on the inside and on the back, sealed with seven seals;
2 And I saw a strong angel proclaiming with a loud voice, Who is worthy to open the book, and to loose the seals thereof?	2 and I saw a mighty angel proclaiming with a loud voice, "Who is worthy to open the scroll and break its seals?"
3 And no man in heaven, nor in earth, neither under the earth, was able to open the book, neither to look thereon.	3 And no one in heaven or on earth or under the earth was able to open the scroll or to look into it.
4 And I wept much, because no man was found worthy to open and to read the book, neither to look thereon.	4 And I began to weep bitterly because no one was found worthy to open the scroll or to look into it.

Know It

The book of Revelation has long been revered by Christians. It contains intricate and symbolic language that many people find hard to understand. Even theologians read it with respect, many offering probabilities rather than exact meanings for its words and phrases. Even so, it is the Word of God. Every word that John wrote in this book has the inspiration of the Spirit, just like the rest of the Bible (2 Tim. 3:16). And though there is speculation about the meaning of some parts of Revelation, there are many parts that are clearly understood and meaningful to believers.

The events of Revelation were revealed to John during the latter part of his life. One thing of note is that John lived longer than any of Jesus' disciples, and because of his faithfulness to Jesus, he was exiled to the isle of Patmos (Rev. 1:9). While there, Jesus visited John, choosing him to come to heaven and witness "what must take place" (Rev. 4:1) on earth. John, who is in the Spirit (4:2), is taken to the throne room of God and sees God seated on His throne. What an honor this must have been! The Bible refers to John as the one whom Jesus loved—indicating a close relationship between him and Jesus. Whether John has been favored with the privilege of receiving this heavenly vision is only speculation.

In our passage, John notices God is holding something important in His right hand. It is a scroll with writing on both sides and sealed with seven seals. John notices every detail because each one is important for what is happening around him. Some wonder if the scroll in God's hand is like the one Ezekiel was commanded to eat (see Eze. 2:9–10). This is something that can be debated. The detail of the writing on the scroll might also be questioned: How did someone write on the outside of the scroll? Traditionally, a rolled–up sheet of paper would not provide the stability on which someone could write on both sides. It was a scroll like none other, we might say.

There were many angels in heaven and one of them stepped forward seeking to enlist someone to break the seals of the scroll and open it. This angel may have been Gabriel because he performed many tasks for God (see e.g. Luke 1:19), but this cannot be substantiated. The others in the throne room included twenty-four elders and four living creatures. They surrounded the throne, but not one of them stepped forward to open the scroll because they were not worthy. This was devastating to John; he cried and cried. His fear was that no one would know what God had planned for humanity.

2. Worthy Is the Lamb (Revelation 5:5–6)

King James Version	NRSVue
5 And one of the elders saith unto me, Weep not: behold, the Lion of the tribe of Judah, the Root of David, hath prevailed to open the book, and to loose the seven seals thereof.	**5** Then one of the elders said to me, "Do not weep. See, the Lion of the tribe of Judah, the Root of David, has conquered, so that he can open the scroll and its seven seals."
6 And I beheld, and, lo, in the midst of the throne and of the four beasts, and in the midst of the elders, stood a Lamb as it had been slain, having seven horns and seven eyes, which are the seven Spirits of God sent forth into all the earth.	**6** Then I saw between the throne and the four living creatures and among the elders a Lamb standing as if it had been slaughtered, having seven horns and seven eyes, which are the seven spirits of God sent out into all the earth.

All was not lost. Through his tears, John saw one of the twenty-four elders answer the question asked by the mighty angel in verse 2. He tells John to stop crying; someone has been found worthy to open the scroll. There is no guessing who this could be. We know beyond a shadow of a doubt that only Jesus is the Worthy One. He is worthy because He is the God–Man, the promised Messiah, the Lamb of God. He is worthy because He did what God sent Him to do. Jesus put Himself into the hands of evil and injustice and was willingly humiliated by humanity. He was whipped mercilessly and brutally nailed to the cross. He willingly laid down His life and went to be killed like a sheep going to be slaughtered. In His suffering and death, Jesus satisfied the wrath of God that was for us. Though we were the ones who deserved the cross, Jesus drank the cup of God's wrath. The One who is worthy, the conquering King, has arrived to take the scroll from the hand of His Father.

The elder calls Jesus "the Lion of the tribe of Judah, the Root of David" (v. 5). This is the first use of these names to describe Jesus, even though there are similar names used. In Jacob's blessing upon his sons, he said, "You are a lion's cub, O Judah," referring to the descendent of David (Gen. 49:9). Then in Isaiah 11:10, the coming Messiah is called the ancestor, or "root of Jesse." Here, the two titles used by the elder point in the direction of Jesus being the royal lion from Judah.

But John did not see a lion; he saw a Lamb. Though He had been crucified on a cross, He was very much alive. John sees Jesus in the center of the throne, surrounded by the elders and the four living creatures. Jesus looks as if He had been slain. During that time, people knew what slain animals looked like. The appearance of a slaughtered animal reminds us of the death of Jesus. The Lamb John saw had seven horns. Lambs do not have horns, so clearly what John witnessed was beyond anything he had seen on earth. In the Old Testament, horns often symbolized power, and the number seven symbolizes completion throughout Scripture. So, seven horns suggest the fullness of divine power. John also sees that the Lamb has seven eyes, which are said to be the seven spirits of God, representing God's truth and omnipresence (Rev. 4:5; Zech. 4:10).

3. Praise to the Worthy One (Revelation 5:7–10)

King James Version	New Revised Standard Version
7 And he came and took the book out of the right hand of him that sat upon the throne.	**7** He went and took the scroll from the right hand of the one who was seated on the throne.
8 And when he had taken the book, the four beasts and four and twenty elders fell down before the Lamb, having every one of them harps, and golden vials full of odours, which are the prayers of saints.	**8** When he had taken the scroll, the four living creatures and the twenty-four elders fell before the Lamb, each holding a harp and golden bowls full of incense, which are the prayers of the saints.
9 And they sung a new song, saying, Thou art worthy to take the book, and to open the seals thereof: for thou wast slain, and hast redeemed us to God by thy blood out of every kindred, and tongue, and people, and nation;	**9** They sing a new song: "You are worthy to take the scroll and to open its seals, for you were slaughtered and by your blood you ransomed for God saints from every tribe and language and people and nation;
10 And hast made us unto our God kings and priests: and we shall reign on the earth.	**10** you have made them to be a kingdom and priests serving our God, and they will reign on earth."

John continues to watch what is happening around him. The Lamb takes the scroll from God with no hesitation or delay. This shows that the Lamb is worthy and able to unleash what is contained in and on the scroll. John probably found peace in knowing Jesus was worthy to open the scroll. When the Lamb takes the scroll, the immediate response of the twenty-four elders is to worship the Lamb. Note that formerly they fell and worshiped God (4:10), who sat on the throne, but this time the elders fell down and worshiped the Lamb.

It is quite a worship service going on in heaven. Each of the twenty four elders worship holding a harp that we can only assume must have also been an instrument of praise during their worship. During biblical times, the harp was a stringed instrument that was well received and encouraged for use in worship (see e.g. Ps. 98:5–6). Most churches today use several different instruments in worship. These instruments create an atmosphere for making a joyful noise to the Lord.

John also saw—and perhaps smelled—golden bowls full of incense. We can imagine the sights and sounds as well as the smells of heaven. Incense was offered at the tabernacle of the Israelites (Exod. 30:7). David compared his prayers to the smoke of incense rising to God (Ps. 141:2). When believers praise and pray to Christ, their worship and prayers are received by Christ in heaven. This visual of the rising incense smoke helps to strengthen the faith of believers. It indicates our prayers not only reach the throne of God, but He hears them. What John sees is symbolic; our prayers really do reach the throne of God.

Everyone in the throne room focuses their attention on Jesus because He takes the scroll and can open its seals. The words in the song confirm the Lamb's worthiness because of the sacrifice He made for our sins. The song also testifies that the redemptive work of Christ is not only for Jews, but for everyone. Those who receive Christ will be counted as members of the priesthood of God (1 Pet. 2:9). For what Christ has done on the cross and for God's acceptance of us into His priesthood, worship should forever be on our lips. God's love is great and without end. He demonstrated this when He gave up His Son, who obediently died in our place. Everyone in heaven focuses praise toward God, then to His Son. They are worthy to be honored and praised.

Remember It

Jesus Christ is the only One in heaven who can take the scroll and open its seals. He is the only One worthy and able to unfold God's plan for all of humanity. God's plan included the price Jesus paid when He died on the cross and rose again from the dead. Because of Jesus' sacrifice and resurrection, heaven will one day be our eternal home. Surely, we should join in God's everlasting plan. We can do so by choosing to praise Jesus Christ. We can participate on earth with the twenty-four elders in our day-to-day lives, letting our praise and worship rise to heaven. One day the wonderful time will come when not only us, but also every creature will praise God and the Lamb forever.

• • • • • • • • • • • • • • • • • •

Share It • Live It • Hear It

Inspired by Revelation 19:12, Matthew Bridges wrote the original lyrics for the song "Crown Him with Many Crowns." Use music software or an online search engine to find a version of this song. Read Revelation 19:12 and meditate on the lyrics.

The redemptive work of Christ made Him the worthy One. The most important way we can honor Jesus is to be part of a church that is committed to worshiping Jesus Christ as a primary goal. What does your commitment look like?

Jesus commanded us to share what He has done with others. We should not allow prejudice to cause us to pick and choose with whom to share. God loves the whole world and wants everyone to be saved (John 3:16). Share the Gospel message with someone today.

Get Social

Start an online conversation about **#WORSHIP**.
Share your views and tag us @rhboydco and use #rhboydco.

@rhboydco

DDR

Devotional Readings for April 24–28, 2025

	MONDAY	TUESDAY	WEDNESDAY	THURSDAY	FRIDAY	SATURDAY	SUNDAY
	Answer Me, O Lord	Be Alert	The Lord Will Not Reject Forever	God Patiently Waits for Repentance	Live the Godly Life	A Presumptive King	A Costly Sacrifice
	Psalm 86:1-7, 10–17	1 Peter 5	Lamentations 3:21–36	2 Peter 3:1–10	2 Peter 3:11–18	1 Chronicles 21:1–13	1 Chronicles 21:14–30

IT'LL COST YOU EVERYTHING

BACKGROUND PASSAGE: 1 CHRONICLES 21:1–22:1
PRINT PASSAGE: 1 CHRONICLES 21:14–30

RESOURCES: *New National Baptist Hymnal 21st Century Edition,*
Boyd's Commentary for the Sunday School

KEY VERSE: And king David said to Ornan, Nay; but I will verily buy it for the full price: for I will not take that which is thine for the Lord, nor offer burnt offerings without cost. (1 Chronicles 21:24, KJV)

Intro

Credit cards can be both a blessing and a curse. The blessing of credit cards is the convenience of making purchases without cash. Gas, groceries, household supplies, and even high-priced items such as televisions and appliances can be purchased with ease. Other benefits are attached to credit cards as well—like reward incentives and building or rebuilding your credit. The user may accumulate points, perks, and even get cash back if the credit is used responsibly. Once one is deemed trustworthy, they may be offered more incentives or a higher credit limit. But that's where the curse might come in.

Using credit cards irresponsibly means overextending one's debts. Some people use the credit card to suit their fancy by shopping excessively, eating at elegant restaurants, treating friends, and more. Repeat spending with the use of a credit card can create a mountain of unpayable debt. Because of this, abusive credit users sometimes must take drastic measures to avoid penalties and a damaged credit score. In the end, they end up losing almost everything because of greed and a lack of wisdom. This is a hard lesson that many have endured, including King David. God has set up standards for taking a census, but David decided to do it his way. In essence, David chose to irresponsibly abuse the Law of God. Pridefully, David did not pay any attention to the blessings God promised him if he obeyed. When God disciplined David, it almost cost him everything.

Think About It

God disciplines those whom He loves (Heb. 12:6), and His correction can be costly, sometimes requiring us to lose nearly everything. How does this transform our hearts, renew our minds, and reshape our lives?

_____

_____

1. God's Plague of Destruction (1 Chronicles 21:14–17)

King James Version	NRSVue
SO the Lord sent pestilence upon Israel: and there fell of Israel seventy thousand men.	SO the Lord sent a pestilence on Israel; and seventy thousand persons fell in Israel.
15 And God sent an angel unto Jerusalem to destroy it: and as he was destroying, the Lord beheld, and he repented him of the evil, and said to the angel that destroyed, It is enough, stay now thine hand. And the angel of the Lord stood by the threshingfloor of Ornan the Jebusite.	15 And God sent an angel to Jerusalem to destroy it; but when he was about to destroy it, the Lord took note and relented concerning the calamity; he said to the destroying angel, "Enough! Stay your hand." The angel of the Lord was then standing by the threshing floor of Ornan the Jebusite.
16 And David lifted up his eyes, and saw the angel of the Lord stand between the earth and the heaven, having a drawn sword in his hand stretched out over Jerusalem. Then David and the elders of Israel, who were clothed in sackcloth, fell upon their faces.	16 David looked up and saw the angel of the Lord standing between earth and heaven, and in his hand a drawn sword stretched out over Jerusalem. Then David and the elders, clothed in sackcloth, fell on their faces.
17 And David said unto God, Is it not I that commanded the people to be numbered? even I it is that have sinned and done evil indeed; but as for these sheep, what have they done? let thine hand, I pray thee, O Lord my God, be on me, and on my father's house; but not on thy people, that they should be plagued.	17 And David said to God, "Was it not I who gave the command to count the people? It is I who have sinned and done very wickedly. But these sheep, what have they done? Let your hand, I pray, O Lord my God, be against me and against my father's house; but do not let your people be plagued!"

Know It

King David, the man after God's own heart (1 Sam. 13:14), was not perfect. There were times when he lost his focus and followed his own heart or when he yielded to the temptations of Satan. This was the case when David ignored God's instructions related to taking a census. God's law had stipulated that each person who was counted had to make a payment of a half shekel to the Temple treasury. God would send a plague if these directions were not followed (see Exod. 30:11–16).

This was serious, yet David chose to listen to the promptings of Satan, who told David to count the people (1 Chron. 21:1). Going his own way, David demonstrates a lack of trust in God. This was significant because it shows that, in the event of a battle, David trusts in the number of his soldiers rather than in the presence of his mighty God. David instructs Joab, his commander, to carry out the census. God was not pleased with David's disobedience. David humbly acknowledges his sin. However, there are consequences; God has to punish David for this sin.

We serve a God who does not lie. He will do what He has promised. A plague was promised. But God, in His mercy, gives David three choices. It was a horrible list of alternatives. David had to pick whether he wanted three years of famine, three months of devastation by his foes, or three days of the sword of the Lord—which was a plague (v. 11). David chose the plague. It did not matter which option he chose, David and God's people would suffer. Disobedience to God often results in dire consequences.

2. David's Altar Built (1 Chronicles 21:18–25)

King James Version	NRSVue
18 Then the angel of the Lord commanded Gad to say to David, that David should go up, and set up an altar unto the Lord in the threshingfloor of Ornan the Jebusite.	**18** Then the angel of the Lord commanded Gad to tell David that he should go up and erect an altar to the Lord on the threshing floor of Ornan the Jebusite.
19 And David went up at the saying of Gad, which he spake in the name of the Lord.	**19** So David went up following Gad's instructions, which he had spoken in the name of the Lord.
20 And Ornan turned back, and saw the angel; and his four sons with him hid themselves. Now Ornan was threshing wheat.	**20** Ornan turned and saw the angel; and while his four sons who were with him hid themselves, Ornan continued to thresh wheat.
21 And as David came to Ornan, Ornan looked and saw David, and went out of the threshingfloor, and bowed himself to David with his face to the ground.	**21** As David came to Ornan, Ornan looked and saw David; he went out from the threshing floor, and did obeisance to David with his face to the ground.
22 Then David said to Ornan, Grant me the place of this threshingfloor, that I may build an altar therein unto the Lord: thou shalt grant it me for the full price: that the plague may be stayed from the people.	**22** David said to Ornan, "Give me the site of the threshing floor that I may build on it an altar to the Lord—give it to me at its full price—so that the plague may be averted from the people."
23 And Ornan said unto David, Take it to thee, and let my lord the king do that which is good in his eyes: lo, I give thee the oxen also for burnt offerings, and the threshing instruments for wood, and the wheat for the meat offering; I give it all.	**23** Then Ornan said to David, "Take it; and let my lord the king do what seems good to him; see, I present the oxen for burnt offerings, and the threshing sledges for the wood, and the wheat for a grain offering. I give it all."

2. David's Altar Built (1 Chronicles 21:18–25, Cont'd)

King James Version	NRSVue
24 And king David said to Ornan, Nay; but I will verily buy it for the full price: for I will not take that which is thine for the Lord, nor offer burnt offerings without cost.	**24** But King David said to Ornan, "No; I will buy them for the full price. I will not take for the Lord what is yours, nor offer burnt offerings that cost me nothing."
25 So David gave to Ornan for the place six hundred shekels of gold by weight.	**25** So David paid Ornan six hundred shekels of gold by weight for the site.

The angel obeys God and stops using the sword that was causing the plague. Earlier, God had spoken to David through David's seer, Gad, who revealed the three choices of punishment to David. This time, in the presence of the powerful angel, through Gad, God tells David to build an altar. The Israelites built altars to meet with and worship God. So, the presence of an altar represented the presence of God. David had committed an egregious sin that required consecration.

God directs David to erect the altar on the threshing floor of Ornan (v. 18). This was the very spot where the angel was standing (v. 15). David agreed. At this point, it's certain that he would have done just about anything to make amends for what he had done. It seems that Ornan did not notice what was going on around him (v. 20). He and his sons were busily at work, threshing wheat. But when they looked up, they got the shock of their lives. There stood a menacing being—the angel of God with a sword. Ornan's sons hide, as would most anyone would have done (v. 20). However, Ornan sees David approaching. With a king in his presence, Ornan did what was expected and bowed to David with his face to the ground (v. 21).

David told Ornan the reason he was there. He wanted to purchase the threshing floor plot from Ornan so that he could build an altar in obedience to God. The threshing floor that Ornan owned already had a rich history. It was located on Mount Moriah, where Abraham offered Isaac as a sacrifice (2 Chron. 3:1–4, Gen. 22:2). David wanted to purchase the plot at full market price. His reason? He wanted the plague on the Israelites to stop. But Ornan's response is to gift the land to David; if David wants to build an altar on his threshing floor, he could have it. Ornan was happy to give David everything needed: the plot, the meat, the wood, the grain—whatever David needed for a sacrifice. After all, this was the king.

Despite Ornan's generosity, however, this was not the way for David. It would have been nonsense for David to perform a sacrifice to God to atone for his sin if he used what somebody else placed at his disposal. David did not want to offer a sacrifice on an altar that did not cost him nothing. So, David pays Ornan what the threshing floor was worth—six hundred shekels of gold (v. 25).

3. David's Sacrifices Accepted (1 Chronicles 21:26–30)

King James Version	New Revised Standard Version
26 And David built there an altar unto the Lord, and offered burnt offerings and peace offerings, and called upon the Lord; and he answered him from heaven by fire upon the altar of burnt offering.	**26** David built there an altar to the Lord and presented burnt offerings and offerings of well-being. He called upon the Lord, and he answered him with fire from heaven on the altar of burnt offering.
27 And the Lord commanded the angel; and he put up his sword again into the sheath thereof.	**27** Then the Lord commanded the angel, and he put his sword back into its sheath.
28 At that time when David saw that the Lord had answered him in the threshingfloor of Ornan the Jebusite, then he sacrificed there.	**28** At that time, when David saw that the Lord had answered him at the threshing floor of Ornan the Jebusite, he made his sacrifices there.
29 For the tabernacle of the Lord, which Moses made in the wilderness, and the altar of the burnt offering, were at that season in the high place at Gibeon.	**29** For the tabernacle of the Lord, which Moses had made in the wilderness, and the altar of burnt offering were at that time in the high place at Gibeon;
30 But David could not go before it to enquire of God: for he was afraid because of the sword of the angel of the Lord.	**30** but David could not go before it to inquire of God, for he was afraid of the sword of the angel of the Lord.

David builds the altar and performs the sacrifice. Obviously, time must have passed between David's initial visit to the threshing floor and when everything was ready for the sacrifice. By this time, other people, such as priests, were probably present, and still the menacing angel loomed above the scene. When David made the offerings, two things happened. God reveals His acceptance of David's sacrifice by sending fire down on the altar and the angel sheaths his sword. Both of these things were most certainly a relief for David. He probably kneeled with bated breath in anticipation of what God would do when he made the sacrifice.

David had lost his way, unwisely disobeying God by issuing a census. Because of this one act of disobedience, it almost costs David everything. His people were subjected to a violent plague at the hands of God's massive angel. But God's disapproval was satisfied, and the plague stopped. David, whom God said was a man after His own heart, was restored in his standing with God. David designates the altar at Ornan's threshing floor as the official site for royal sacrifices. The central place of worship for all Israel was located in the tabernacle at Gibeon. But despite David's restoration, he had been traumatized; David continues to worship at the threshing floor because he was afraid of the sword of God's angel.

Remember It

David conducted a census that brought disaster on him and those for whom he was responsible. He did not follow God's commands related to carrying out a census. Instead, David pridefully wanted to see the size of his army. At this point, he trusted more in military power than in the power of God. Even though David realized his sin, the deed had been done. The harsh punishment of a plague was chosen by David, when God gave him three options. But God, in His mercy, stopped the plague and invited David to build an altar. David's offering was pleasing to God. This is a story of God's grace and love—both of which were demonstrated when God restored His servant, David.

● ● ● ● ● ● ● ● ● ● ● ● ● ● ● ● ● ●

Share It • Live It • Hear It

While listening to soft praise and worship music, reflect on whether sin in your life has cost you almost everything. If so, pause to offer a prayer of repentance. Let your worship be what (metaphorically) builds an altar for the presence of God.

There is a thin line between what God does for us and what we pridefully do for ourselves. Sometimes, we even foolishly claim a move of our own as a move of God. We should choose to obey God in all things to avoid facing God's discipline.

When you see pride lived out in another believer's life, share the story of David's census event and urge them to seek God for forgiveness. Remind others that God's forgiveness is guaranteed to redeem us but that does not always mean there will not be natural consequences with which we must deal.

Get Social
Start an online conversation about **#OBEDIENCE**.
Share your views and tag us @rhboydco and use #rhboydco.

@rhboydco

DDR

Devotional Readings for May 5–11, 2025

MONDAY	TUESDAY	WEDNESDAY	THURSDAY	FRIDAY	SATURDAY	SUNDAY
A Joyful Celebration	God Heard Me in My Distress	God in Mesopotamia	God in the Wilderness	God Needs No Temple	Hear Our Prayers, O God	God's Glory Fills the Temple
Ezra 6:14–22	Psalm 18:1–12	Acts 7:2–16	Acts 7:30–41	Acts 7:42–50	2 Chronicles 6:12, 14–27	2 Chronicles 7:1–7, 11

A GRAND OPENING

BACKGROUND PASSAGE: 2 CHRONICLES 7:1–20
PRINT PASSAGE: 2 CHRONICLES 7:1–7, 11

RESOURCES: *New National Baptist Hymnal 21st Century Edition,*
Boyd's Commentary for the Sunday School

KEY VERSE: When all the people of Israel saw the fire come down and the glory of the LORD on the temple, they bowed down on the pavement with their faces to the ground, and worshiped and gave thanks to the Lord, saying, "For he is good, for his steadfast love endures forever." (2 Chronicles 7:3, NRSVue)

Intro

Savannah, Georgia's First African Baptist Church is cited as the oldest Black church in North America. Established in 1773, it predates the official formation of our country by three years. From rocky beginnings, First African has withstood the test of time. Initially, its members could not meet because it was against the law for enslaved persons to gather in public places without the supervision of a white person. But after negotiations with the British, the church was allowed to meet. In 1775, Rev. George Liele (also Lisle), the first pastor was allowed to preach. With that as a foundation, First African Baptist Church endured God-led victories that included land purchases, relocations, and building construction. The church was also a critical station on the Underground Railroad; the sanctuary still bears evidence of its involvement.

The experiences of First African congregants are representative of the struggles of Black Christians to establish peaceful places of worship. Despite unfair negotiations to purchase land, destruction of church property, death threats, and murders, the Black Church continues. Each Sunday, Black worshipers stand on the shoulders of Pastor Liele (Lisle) and the founding members of First African as they honor and glorify God for keeping the institution for more than 250 years. Thankfully, God's work through Rev. Liele (Lisle) charted the path for worship in the Black context. But more important than the Black Church and our collective histories is the focus on worship. Like Solomon, we worship God for who He is. Our worship is not about us, but rather, about God, the Creator of heaven, earth, and everything in them.

Think About It

What impact might our corporate worship of God have on our daily lives? What needs to change in our worship to strengthen this impact?

_____

_____

_____

1. Temple Dedication (2 Chronicles 7:1–3)

King James Version	NRSVue
NOW when Solomon had made an end of praying, the fire came down from heaven, and consumed the burnt offering and the sacrifices; and the glory of the Lord filled the house.	WHEN Solomon had ended his prayer, fire came down from heaven and consumed the burnt offering and the sacrifices; and the glory of the Lord filled the temple.
2 And the priests could not enter into the house of the Lord, because the glory of the Lord had filled the Lord's house.	**2** The priests could not enter the house of the Lord, because the glory of the Lord filled the Lord's house.
3 And when all the children of Israel saw how the fire came down, and the glory of the Lord upon the house, they bowed themselves with their faces to the ground upon the pavement, and worshipped, and praised the Lord, saying, For he is good; for his mercy endureth for ever.	**3** When all the people of Israel saw the fire come down and the glory of the Lord on the temple, they bowed down on the pavement with their faces to the ground, and worshiped and gave thanks to the Lord, saying, "For he is good, for his steadfast love endures forever."

Know It

The history of the Israelite Temple included the desire of a king and a denial from God. Because of his allegiance to God, David had a strong desire to build a house for his Lord (1 Kings 8:18). But God denied David of this request and gave that responsibility to David's son, Solomon (1 Kings 8:19). So, in obedience to God and through the godly wisdom with which he was blessed, Solomon built the Temple for the Lord. As described in 1 Kings 6, it was a massive structure with beveled window frames, side chambers, and ledges all around the outside. Solomon made sure the Temple was paneled with planks of cedar and overlaid the floors with cypress boards, then overlaid that with gold. The inner sanctuary was the most spectacular. Everything was layered with gold, including the bronze altar and the carved cherubim. God was certainly honored by the work and craftsmanship. Solomon led in the construction of a sacred building that honored and glorified the One who Himself skillfully created the entire world.

After Solomon finished building the Temple, he dedicated it to God. Dedication meant the Temple's activities would be completely devoted to God. Solomon's dedication prayer was a long and detailed prayer of praise for who God is and for what He had done. It was a prayer of repentance. It was a prayer of intercession and petition. And it was a prayer of deep submission. Solomon covered all of life's bases. Everything needed to be covered if God was to live in the Temple among the people.

After Solomon finished his prayer, God responded with an overwhelming demonstration of His presence. Fire came down from heaven and consumed the sacrifices. It was God's confirming response of acceptance to Solomon's dedication and the offerings. The Temple was in the same spot of David's altar on Ornan's threshing floor. The divine fire descended from heaven as well.

Everyone responded to the demonstration of God's glory by bowing down in worship with their faces to the ground. When we bow before the Lord, we acknowledge God's greatness and our insufficiency. God is great in every sense of the word "great." He is great in love, great in power, great in wisdom, great in splendor, and great in majesty. In fact, God's greatness cannot be compared to anything on earth (Ps. 145:3). When the Israelites honored God, they used the well-known liturgical phrase, "For the Lord is good; his steadfast love endures forever" (Ps. 100:5). It was the hallelujah event for the ages.

2. Temple Dedication Celebrated (2 Chronicles 7:4–7)

King James Version	NRSVue
4 Then the king and all the people offered sacrifices before the Lord.	4 Then the king and all the people offered sacrifice before the Lord.
5 And king Solomon offered a sacrifice of twenty and two thousand oxen, and an hundred and twenty thousand sheep: so the king and all the people dedicated the house of God.	5 King Solomon offered as a sacrifice twenty-two thousand oxen and one hundred twenty thousand sheep. So the king and all the people dedicated the house of God.
6 And the priests waited on their offices: the Levites also with instruments of musick of the Lord, which David the king had made to praise the Lord, because his mercy endureth for ever, when David praised by their ministry; and the priests sounded trumpets before them, and all Israel stood.	6 The priests stood at their posts, the Levites also, with the instruments for music to the Lord that King David had made for giving thanks to the Lord—for his steadfast love endures forever—whenever David offered praises by their playing. Opposite them the priests sounded trumpets, and all Israel stood.
7 Moreover Solomon hallowed the middle of the court that was before the house of the Lord: for there he offered burnt offerings, and the fat of the peace offerings, because the brasen altar which Solomon had made was not able to receive the burnt offerings, and the meat offerings, and the fat.	7 Solomon consecrated the middle of the court that was in front of the house of the Lord; for there he offered the burnt offerings and the fat of the offerings of well-being because the bronze altar Solomon had made could not hold the burnt offering and the grain offering and the fat parts.

When the fire came down from heaven, no one ran away in fear. Instead, God's response made it clear that the Lord approved of the Temple and its dedication prayer from Solomon. With God's approval, the first sacrificial services could be conducted; and with the completion of the Temple, everything was ready. God was praised and honored with worship. But despite the praise and worship that took place, this could not replace required sacrificial offerings to God. And what sacrifices they were! Solomon conducted the sacrifice of 22,000 oxen and 120,000 sheep. The details of how this was accomplished are not provided, but the sacrifice of so many animals required organization. Maybe an assembly-style, mass slaughter was used to handle this large offering. Everyone had their own responsibilities to ensure that each animal was ritually sacrificed. The practice was to dedicate a portion to God and a portion to the priests and the people in attendance. They had enough food so that no one went hungry during the fifteen days of celebration (see vv. 8–10).

The fire that came from heaven was the evidence that God had accepted Solomon's prayer. The Holy Spirit provides the surest evidence that God accepts our prayers as believers. Not only does the Spirit assist us with prayer, but since we have been given the amazing gift of God's Spirit inside ourselves, we can comprehend the thoughts of God (1 Cor. 2:10–11).

During this celebration, Solomon consecrated the middle of the courtyard (v. 7). He could not conduct the sacrificial service in the Temple, but rather had to take the offerings outside because of the number of the animals to be sacrificed. It was right that he consecrated the outside area first. To "consecrate" something means it is made pure, so that it will not offend our holy God. Sometimes, the people had to consecrate themselves by bathing and washing their clothes so that they would not contaminate their relationship with God. Everything at the celebration had to be pleasing to God. We must consecrate ourselves when we have been contaminated by the world or its things. We primarily do this through prayers of confession and repentance. God has called us to be holy because He is holy (1 Peter 1:15–16).

The Levites with musical instruments continued to praise God, and the priests joined in with their trumpets. They were joined by all Israel. It was a joyous occasion as they praised God using instruments that King David had made for worship. But the celebration had to come to an end, and finally Solomon sent the people home (v. 10). They adjourned with joy in their hearts and gratitude to God for what he had done.

3. Temple Dedication Finished (2 Chronicles 7:11)

King James Version	NRSVue
11 Thus Solomon finished the house of the Lord, and the king's house: and all that came into Solomon's heart to make in the house of the Lord, and in his own house, he prosperously effected.	11 Thus Solomon finished the house of the Lord and the king's house; all that Solomon had planned to do in the house of the Lord and in his own house he successfully accomplished.

NOTES:

Solomon's reign began with a sincere desire to be pleasing to God. He is renowned for asking for wisdom so that he could wisely rule God's people. This revealed to God that Solomon had his priorities in order. Therefore, God gave Solomon wealth, riches, and honor as well. Jesus also spoke about priorities. He said when we put God first, everything we need for an obedient life in service to Him would be provided (Matt. 6:33). This does not mean we will receive riches like Solomon—that's at God's sovereign discretion. But it does mean we will be cared for.

Because of the wisdom and gifts God had given to Solomon, he achieved much as king. Building the Temple was only one of many of his accomplishments. Solomon also built a royal palace for himself. It took Solomon twenty years to build the Temple as well as his place (1 Kings 6:38–7:11), and the writer of 2 Chronicles declared it successful (v. 11). Following the building of the Temple, God promised that He would establish Solomon's kingdom if he fully did all that God commanded (vv. 17–18). However, if Solomon proved unfaithful, God's people would go into exile, and the Temple would be destroyed (vv. 19–22). This shows how to avoid the consequences of disobedience. It is applicable to us today.

But Solomon built a beautiful Temple and lived in peace. The Temple became the religious center of the nation of Israel. It symbolized unity among the tribes and the presence of their great God. This massive endeavor rose out of the heart of Solomon who committed his life and work to follow and honor God.

Remember It

Solomon, in obedience and dedication to God, built a magnificent Temple for God. At that time, it was a necessary building where people could meet with God and worship Him. Solomon did everything necessary for this endeavor. Artisans and materials of highest quality, including gold, was chosen—nothing but the best for God. Then, Solomon did what was most important: he dedicated the Temple through prayer. God communicated His approval and acceptance as He rained down fire on Solomon's offering. Today, God doesn't need magnificent buildings or facilities—we are the temple of the Holy Spirit (1 Cor. 6:19)—but He does still require our dedication in worship.

• • • • • • • • • • • • • • • • • • •

Share It • Live It • Hear It

Choose and listen to a celebratory gospel song. As you listen, celebrate God's presence in your life through the Holy Spirit. Share with class members how you know you are the temple of God and in what ways you live out the lyrics of your chosen Gospel song.

God isn't concerned with the size of church buildings nearly as much as He cares about our hearts. God wants us to take good care of ourselves. This includes our body, mind, and spirit. God desires that we grow mightily to reflect the image of the Son.

Choose a person with whom you can share the Gospel this week. When you share, let them know they will receive God's Holy Spirit. They won't have to be alone in this wicked world.

𝕏 ⓘ f
@rhboydco

DDR

Devotional Readings for May 12–18, 2025

	MONDAY	TUESDAY	WEDNESDAY	THURSDAY	FRIDAY	SATURDAY	SUNDAY
	Joy Comes with the Morning	Songs of Gratitude	Blessed Be the Merciful, Consoling God	Enter God's Presence with Thanksgiving	Worship in the Spirit of God	The Exiles Return	Building a New Foundation
	Psalm 30	Colossians 3:12–17	2 Corinthians 1:2–14	Psalm 95	Philippians 3:1–14	Ezra 1	Ezra 3:1–6, 10–13

MOURNING THE PAST OR CELEBRATING THE FUTURE?

BACKGROUND PASSAGE: EZRA 3:1–13   **PRINT PASSAGE: EZRA 3:1–6, 10–13**

RESOURCES: *New National Baptist Hymnal 21st Century Edition, Boyd's Commentary for the Sunday School*

KEY VERSE: And they sang together by course in praising and giving thanks unto the Lord; because he is good, for his mercy endureth for ever toward Israel. And all the people shouted with a great shout, when they praised the Lord, because the foundation of the house of the Lord was laid. (Ezra 3:11, KJV)

Intro

Every generation can look back to "good old days"—a period when past life experiences seemed better than present day times. Sometimes this reminiscence can become obsessive if *old* days overtake *new* ones. Consider the Silent Generation—those born between 1925 and 1945. Even though there are people still alive who are older, this demographic is considered to be the oldest people living. Reflecting on the "good old days" for this age group, we learn that they lived through two wars and the Great Depression. Today, while there seems to be little respect for authority, the Silent Generation had deep respect for leaders. While immorality is slowly becoming the norm, the majority of those in the Silent Generation was committed to their churches and religious beliefs. While many in today's culture highly value a life of ease, the Silent Generation believed that hard work was its own reward. Those rewards became the "good" of *all* days.

People of the Silent Generation are today's parents, grandparents, and great–grandparents who might remember and speak about "the way things were." In remembering "good old days," they might mourn over trends of the current day. In a similar way, the people in today's text who had witnessed the magnificence of Solomon's Temple wept as they recalled the "good old days." When the Jerusalem Temple was destroyed, it was eventually rebuilt, though not to its former glory. As believers, rather than long for the "good old days," we are encouraged to seek God's hand in every change. In so doing, we find joy in every day.

Think About It

How can we live in light of eternity by focusing forward, rather than backward, on the work God has called us to do?

_____

_____

_____

1. Worship God Despite Fear (Ezra 3:1–3)

King James Version	NRSVue
AND when the seventh month was come, and the children of Israel were in the cities, the people gathered themselves together as one man to Jerusalem.	WHEN the seventh month came, and the Israelites were in the towns, the people gathered together in Jerusalem.
2 Then stood up Jeshua the son of Jozadak, and his brethren the priests, and Zerubbabel the son of Shealtiel, and his brethren, and builded the altar of the God of Israel, to offer burnt offerings thereon, as it is written in the law of Moses the man of God.	2 Then Jeshua son of Jozadak, with his fellow priests, and Zerubbabel son of Shealtiel with his kin set out to build the altar of the God of Israel, to offer burnt offerings on it, as prescribed in the law of Moses the man of God.
3 And they set the altar upon his bases; for fear was upon them because of the people of those countries: and they offered burnt offerings thereon unto the Lord, even burnt offerings morning and evening.	3 They set up the altar on its foundation, because they were in dread of the neighboring peoples, and they offered burnt offerings upon it to the Lord, morning and evening.

Know It

Ezra was one of the leaders that helped bring the Israelites out of Babylonian captivity. He was a scribe and priest who led the people in worshiping God. The first six chapters of the book of Ezra narrate the first return from exile as well as the rebuilding of the temple. This first group of Jewish people were small in number and faced many problems, but they recognized they must honor God by putting first things first.

Even though Ezra, who reported these events, do not appear personally on the scene until chapter seven of his book, by chapter six the Israelites had settled in their homes. One could imagine how this must have felt for families who had been in captivity for approximately seventy years (2 Chron. 36:21). After being in captivity so long, the people probably missed worshiping God together. They longed to offer sacrifices in their own temple, even though the Babylonians had long ago destroyed the great Temple built by King Solomon. They longed to return to their own law and their own traditions.

Therefore, the leaders stepped forward to get done that which was needed to lead the people to make a new start. The leaders included Jeshua and his fellow priests, along with Zerubbabel and his associates. In some churches, people don't often step forward to fill leadership roles. For the most part, some lack the humble commitment required to lead; while some others might misuse the leadership role, making it a vehicle for lifting themselves up. Certainly, leaders must be humble and enlist others to help, which often takes them out of the spotlight. This was evidently what Jeshua and Zerubbabel had done. These two men took it upon themselves to do the hard work of getting started. In accordance with what was required, they decided to build an altar before rebuilding the Temple. This was the same space of the situation in 2 Samuel 24:25, when David built an altar. This means that area was sacred and was the perfect place for honoring God.

The Israelites wanted to begin correctly. Therefore, it was important that they worship God according to that which was written in the Law of Moses. This was important, even though the Israelites were afraid. They recognized their God was mightier than whatever caused them to be afraid. So, courageously they took the risk to worship their omnipotent God and they built an altar on the foundation of the Temple. The sacrifice they made to God was a burnt offering. In a burnt offering, the whole animal is sacrificed as a symbol of total cleansing and commitment to God. Consider that God ordered Abraham to offer his son, Isaac, as a burnt offering and then provided a ram as a replacement (Gen. 22:1–14). God wanted Abraham to be completely devoted to Him more than the allurement of the promise.

2. Worship God as He Prescribes (Ezra 3:4–6)

King James Version	NRSVue
4 They kept also the feast of tabernacles, as it is written, and offered the daily burnt offerings by number, according to the custom, as the duty of every day required;	**4** And they kept the festival of booths, as prescribed, and offered the daily burnt offerings by number according to the ordinance, as required for each day,
5 And afterward offered the continual burnt offering, both of the new moons, and of all the set feasts of the Lord that were consecrated, and of every one that willingly offered a freewill offering unto the Lord.	**5** and after that the regular burnt offerings, the offerings at the new moon and at all the sacred festivals of the Lord, and the offerings of everyone who made a freewill offering to the Lord.
6 From the first day of the seventh month began they to offer burnt offerings unto the Lord. But the foundation of the temple of the Lord was not yet laid.	**6** From the first day of the seventh month they began to offer burnt offerings to the Lord. But the foundation of the temple of the Lord was not yet laid.

With the success of the burnt offerings, the Israelites continue to worship God by celebrating the Feast of Tabernacles, or "festival of booths" (v. 4)—one of the most important religious celebrations on the Jewish calendar. During the Feast of Tabernacles, the people lived for seven days in tents or booths as their ancestors had done when they lived in the desert on their way to the Promised Land. This festival commemorated their ancestors and reminded them of God's protection of their ancestors while in the wilderness. It was a reminder of God's continuing care and their dependence on Him. Having just settled in their home after the exile in Babylon, this festival would have had special significance.

God's people had learned a difficult lesson. They lived in captivity for a long time because of their disobedience to God. They realized that before the exile, they had lived without a deep commitment to God. It may have been a time when their worship was more habitual and when worship did not matter. But this time their sacrifices were from the heart.

Worship from the heart is important in our worship as well. Jesus said we must worship God in spirit and in truth (John 4:23). Furthermore, it's not so much about where we worship as it was for the Israelites, because the Spirit that lives in us is with us everywhere we go. Whether we are at home, church, or even in a park, what matters is that we honor God. The Israelites understood this. Because they built the altar first, they recognized they could worship God even without a Temple. They wanted to be obedient to God, so their worship had to be according to what was written in the Scripture. They were careful to set up and reestablish worship God's way.

3. Worship God for a New Start (Ezra 3:10–13)

King James Version	NRSVue
10 And when the builders laid the foundation of the temple of the Lord, they set the priests in their apparel with trumpets, and the Levites the sons of Asaph with cymbals, to praise the Lord, after the ordinance of David king of Israel.	**10** When the builders laid the foundation of the temple of the Lord, the priests in their vestments were stationed to praise the Lord with trumpets, and the Levites, the sons of Asaph, with cymbals, according to the directions of King David of Israel;
11 And they sang together by course in praising and giving thanks unto the Lord; because he is good, for his mercy endureth for ever toward Israel. And all the people shouted with a great shout, when they praised the Lord, because the foundation of the house of the Lord was laid.	**11** and they sang responsively, praising and giving thanks to the Lord, "For he is good, for his steadfast love endures forever toward Israel." And all the people responded with a great shout when they praised the Lord, because the foundation of the house of the Lord was laid.

King James Version	New Revised Standard Version
12 But many of the priests and Levites and chief of the fathers, who were ancient men, that had seen the first house, when the foundation of this house was laid before their eyes, wept with a loud voice; and many shouted aloud for joy:	**12** But many of the priests and Levites and heads of families, old people who had seen the first house on its foundations, wept with a loud voice when they saw this house, though many shouted aloud for joy,
13 So that the people could not discern the noise of the shout of joy from the noise of the weeping of the people: for the people shouted with a loud shout, and the noise was heard afar off.	**13** so that the people could not distinguish the sound of the joyful shout from the sound of the people's weeping, for the people shouted so loudly that the sound was heard far away.

Worship was the center of the Israelite community. Soon the time arrived when the foundation of the Temple had been laid. This was a difficult undertaking that required hard work and a joint effort of multiple generations. The current generation of Israelites restored all the elements of worship that had been instituted in previous generations. The priests, who dressed for leading worship, blew trumpets and the Levites joined in with cymbals. Then the people praised God with a joyful noise because the foundation of the Temple had been laid.

The Israelites' shouts of praise were fitting; it was an historic moment that was seventy years in the making. Even though construction had just begun, they were filled with praise at the prospect of seeing God's Temple soon completed. Ezra provides an emotional account of the events that were taking place. Israelites of all ages gather for this time of celebration—children, youth, adults, and senior adults. As in any event, there are different perspectives and emotions present. Noted especially is the response of the older adults, which includes the older priests, Levites, and family heads. Because they remembered Solomon's Temple, instead of praising God for the new foundation, they wept. The new foundation was simpler than Solomon's Temple. Solomon's wealth had supported building the first Temple, with cedar, bronze, and gold among some of the luxurious elements used as building materials. The foundation had been overlaid with gold.

The Israelites had lost everything while in captivity, even access to fine resources. Therefore, many shouted for joy, perhaps because they remembered their captivity rather than the former Temple. The rebuilt foundation caused those who were older to weep and long for the "good old days." Perhaps they remembered the splendor of the previous foundation that was overlaid with gold. No matter the perspective, however, building the altar and laying the Temple foundation marked a new beginning for the Israelites.

Remember It

Though there was not yet a Temple, God was enthroned on the praises of Israel. One of the first things the Israelites did when they were freed from Babylonian captivity was worship God. They spent about seventy years in captivity and had a desire to return to the former things. That included reestablishing their relationship with God. So, the first thing they did was build an altar. Some may think they should have rebuilt the Temple first, but it made better sense to honor and worship God because of God's faithful love and care. After offering sacrifices to God, the foundation of the Temple was laid. The response was mixed, but "new" had come. Change had come for the entire Israelite community.

● ● ● ● ● ● ● ● ● ● ● ● ● ● ● ● ●

Share It • Live It • Hear It

For the Israelites, worship was a lifestyle. As a way of establishing a lifestyle of worship, listen regularly to praise and worship music that honors God. We are encouraged to guard our hearts (Prov. 4:20–23). One way to guard our hearts is to guard our ears.

God expects obedience expressed from a heart of devotion. This is what leads us to worship Him in Spirit and truth. Occasionally, we need to begin again to establish worship as a prominent place in our lives. Begin by connecting with God; seek God for God's self. Seek to understand who He is.

Be an encourager when fellow believers long with a broken heart for the "good old days." Honor where they are while, at the same time, guiding them to embrace God's presence, love, and care in their current lives.

𝕏 ⓘ ⓕ
@rhboydco

Devotional Readings for May 19–25, 2025

DDR

	MONDAY A New Covenant	TUESDAY Saved by Grace	WEDNESDAY A New Covenant	THURSDAY Hear the Word of the Lord	FRIDAY Remember God's Salvation	SATURDAY A Better Covenant	SUNDAY Revitalized Worship
	Jeremiah 31:27–34	Ephesians 2:1–10	Luke 22:7–20	Nehemiah 8:1- 3, 5-6, 8–12	Nehemiah 9:2- 3, 6–17, 32	Hebrews 8	Nehemiah 10:28–39

HERE WE GO AGAIN!

BACKGROUND PASSAGE: NEHEMIAH 8:1–10:39
PRINT PASSAGE: NEHEMIAH 10:28–39

> RESOURCES: *New National Baptist Hymnal 21st Century Edition,*
> *Boyd's Commentary for the Sunday School*

KEY VERSE: We will not neglect the house of our God. (Nehemiah 10:39, NRSVue)

Intro

This Old House, a home improvement television show, seeks out homes in need of repair. Their expert cast members execute renovations and restorations of homes to their former glory. Sometimes, the project is extensive, requiring a complete excavation; other times, the work requires only a little paint and a change of flooring. No matter what, every project retains the bones or foundational elements of the restored home. The foundation of a home is a central component. It keeps the house sturdy and provides stability against harsh, climatic elements. With a solid foundation, a house is a safe haven for its inhabitants for many years.

A foundational concept also exists in the Bible. God's covenant with the Israelites was a foundational element that established a relationship. The covenant of God was built on a solid foundation of God's love, mercy, and truth. No matter what occurred between God and the Israelites, the foundation remained intact, just like the foundation of a house. Often, the covenant was violated by the Israelites, who did not live according to the terms of the covenant. This, however, would not change God's covenantal terms, usually including discipline. When the Israelites had enough, they would cry out to God. Because of the foundation on which their relationship was built, God always responded with restoration. Nehemiah led the Israelites in restoration efforts after gaining their freedom. Because of disobedience to God's laws, they spent many years in captivity. Jerusalem was destroyed but God used Nehemiah to restore it.

Think About It

How should we define the foundational covenant that believers have with God? What can we do to keep it strong, especially during times of testing and adversity?

_____

_____

_____

1. Committing to God (Nehemiah 10:28–29)

King James Version	NRSVue
AND the rest of the people, the priests, the Levites, the porters, the singers, the Nethinims, and all they that had separated themselves from the people of the lands unto the law of God, their wives, their sons, and their daughters, every one having knowledge, and having understanding; **29** They clave to their brethren, their nobles, and entered into a curse, and into an oath, to walk in God's law, which was given by Moses the servant of God, and to observe and do all the commandments of the Lord our Lord, and his judgments and his statutes;	THE rest of the people, the priests, the Levites, the gatekeepers, the singers, the temple servants, and all who have separated themselves from the peoples of the lands to adhere to the law of God, their wives, their sons, their daughters, all who have knowledge and understanding, **29** join with their kin, their nobles, and enter into a curse and an oath to walk in God's law, which was given by Moses the servant of God, and to observe and do all the commandments of the Lord our Lord and his ordinances and his statutes.

Know It

The book of Nehemiah deals with Israel's spiritual restoration under Ezra and Nehemiah's shared leadership. With concern about the restoration of the covenant between God and the Israelites, Nehemiah emphasizes that the Israelites should faithfully keep the Torah and rightly worship the Lord. Nehemiah had spiritual gifts that God used to get the job done. With his gifts, Nehemiah took action. Though he was met with opposition, he kept going until the walls were built. Nehemiah understood that God wanted him to lead the Jews to rebuild the torn down walls of Jerusalem. Like Nehemiah, we must faithfully handle whatever spiritual gift God has given us. In this way, the flock of God will reap spiritual blessings and we can reach a dying world for Christ.

Nehemiah 8–10 sets the context for today's lesson. After building the walls, Nehemiah continues to lead the Israelites to restore the foundation of their covenantal relationship with God. Before the covenant is signed, a prayer of praise to God and repentance for sins is voiced (9:7–37). Then a written, binding agreement is placed before the people, and one by one, the Levites and the leaders of the people sign it. It is an agreement that renews their covenant with God. Beyond the Levites and Israelite leaders, wives, husbands, and the entire community of people are involved. This is only right; all the people separated themselves from God and from one another. Therefore, they all need to repent and be restored. Rather than sign, the greater community verbally bind themselves with an oath to follow God's Law.

2. Making a Vow (Nehemiah 10:30–31)

King James Version	NRSVue
30 And that we would not give our daughters unto the people of the land, not take their daughters for our sons: **31** And if the people of the land bring ware or any victuals on the sabbath day to sell, that we would not buy it of them on the sabbath, or on the holy day: and that we would leave the seventh year, and the exaction of every debt.	**30** We will not give our daughters to the peoples of the land or take their daughters for our sons; **31** and if the peoples of the land bring in merchandise or any grain on the sabbath day to sell, we will not buy it from them on the sabbath or on a holy day; and we will forego the crops of the seventh year and the exaction of every debt.

Vows are promises to do specific things. We make marriage or wedding vows, which are a couple's commitment to God and each other. Marriage vows fortify a couple's determination to fight for their relationship when difficulties arise and cements their love and desire to live as one. The Israelites also made a vow related to marriage, but it was a little different in its focus. The Israelites made a promise not to allow their children to marry the people around them. It was God's Law given through Moses. However, this Law had been broken. Throughout their history, the Israelites had been pulled toward foreign practices and were distracted and tempted by foreign customs and possessions. These practices continually got the Israelites into trouble. It was also important to honor God on the Sabbath. It had been established that God's people should not work on the seventh day of the week (Gen. 2:2). We must prioritize God over the money we earn from our jobs, ensuring that our worship habits continue to honor Him.

3. Reestablishing God's Commands (Nehemiah 10:32–39)

King James Version	NRSVue
32 Also we made ordinances for us, to charge ourselves yearly with the third part of a shekel for the service of the house of our God; **33** For the shewbread, and for the continual meat offering, and for the continual burnt offering, of the sabbaths, of the new moons, for the set feasts, and for the holy things, and for the sin offerings to make an atonement for Israel, and for all the work of the house of our God.	**32** We also lay on ourselves the obligation to charge ourselves yearly one-third of a shekel for the service of the house of our God: **33** for the rows of bread, the regular grain offering, the regular burnt offering, the sabbaths, the new moons, the appointed festivals, the sacred donations, and the sin offerings to make atonement for Israel, and for all the work of the house of our God.

3. Reestablishing God's Commands (Nehemiah 10:32–39, Cont'd)

King James Version	New Revised Standard Version
34 And we cast the lots among the priests, the Levites, and the people, for the wood offering, to bring it into the house of our God, after the houses of our fathers, at times appointed year by year, to burn upon the altar of the Lord our God, as it is written in the law:	**34** We have also cast lots among the priests, the Levites, and the people, for the wood offering, to bring it into the house of our God, by ancestral houses, at appointed times, year by year, to burn on the altar of the Lord our God, as it is written in the law.
35 And to bring the firstfruits of our ground, and the firstfruits of all fruit of all trees, year by year, unto the house of the Lord:	**35** We obligate ourselves to bring the first fruits of our soil and the first fruits of all fruit of every tree, year by year, to the house of the Lord;
36 Also the firstborn of our sons, and of our cattle, as it is written in the law, and the firstlings of our herds and of our flocks, to bring to the house of our God, unto the priests that minister in the house of our God:	**36** also to bring to the house of our God, to the priests who minister in the house of our God, the firstborn of our sons and of our livestock, as it is written in the law, and the firstlings of our herds and of our flocks;
37 And that we should bring the firstfruits of our dough, and our offerings, and the fruit of all manner of trees, of wine and of oil, unto the priests, to the chambers of the house of our God; and the tithes of our ground unto the Levites, that the same Levites might have the tithes in all the cities of our tillage.	**37** and to bring the first of our dough, and our contributions, the fruit of every tree, the wine and the oil, to the priests, to the chambers of the house of our God; and to bring to the Levites the tithes from our soil, for it is the Levites who collect the tithes in all our rural towns.
38 And the priest the son of Aaron shall be with the Levites, when the Levites take tithes: and the Levites shall bring up the tithe of the tithes unto the house of our God, to the chambers, into the treasure house.	**38** And the priest, the descendant of Aaron, shall be with the Levites when the Levites receive the tithes; and the Levites shall bring up a tithe of the tithes to the house of our God, to the chambers of the storehouse.
39 For the children of Israel and the children of Levi shall bring the offering of the corn, of the new wine, and the oil, unto the chambers, where are the vessels of the sanctuary, and the priests that minister, and the porters, and the singers: and we will not forsake the house of our God.	**39** For the people of Israel and the sons of Levi shall bring the contribution of grain, wine, and oil to the storerooms where the vessels of the sanctuary are, and where the priests that minister, and the gatekeepers and the singers are. We will not neglect the house of our God.

The Temple tax is not found as a command in the Law; rather, it is the people taking on responsibility to care for God's house. Like any structure or material possession, time causes corrosion and rot. All buildings eventually decay and succumb to the elements if we neglect their care. For this reason, a portion of our church offerings are allocated for the upkeep and sustaining of the building and for replenishing supplies and resources. Similarly, the Israelites agree to pay a third of a shekel each year. By agreeing to this tax, the people assume responsibility for the care and service of the house of God.

The verses state some of the specifics for which the money is collected, which include offerings and celebrations. Several different activities take place in the Temple. Money is required for bread, which is the shewbread. There are twelve loaves that represent the twelve tribes of Israel. They are placed on the table in the Temple as an act of thanksgiving (Lev. 24:5–9). The money is also used for offerings and feasts. These events require daily and annual refreshing of the Temple to keep it clean, uncluttered, and pleasing to God. The Israelites, including the Levites and the priests, set a schedule to distribute the work and assign responsibilities in the Temple. The people cast lots to make distribution of assignments fair. This helped them make decisions when they could not decide who would do what.

Beyond the work, reestablishing their vows to God requires that God receive the first of everything (Exod. 3:19). So once again, the people and the leaders take on the responsibility of bringing the firstfruits of their crop to the Temple. These offerings symbolize God's ownership of everything. In the same way, we tithe ten percent of our income as an act of worship to God, demonstrating our trust that God will provide and, like the Israelites, acknowledging that He owns everything. The people also promise to bring the firstborn of their sons, cattle, herds, and flocks to the house of God. These items, including the sons, are used to maintain sacrifices and care for the priests and the House of God. Numbers 18 specifies that firstborn sons are not to be sacrificed but are to be redeemed by the payment of five shekels of silver (Num. 18:14–17). This money is given to the priests.

The firstborn among unclean animals is also to be redeemed by money paid to the priests. However, the firstborn among the clean animals (ox, sheep, or goats) are to be burned as a holy sacrifice to God. The priests are then given these portions to eat. This was necessary so the priests could continue to minister in the House of God. The vows include how the offerings are to be collected. It is the responsibility of a priest descended from Aaron to accompany the Levites when they receive the tithes. After collection, Levites are to bring a tenth of the tithes up to the house of God, to the storerooms of the treasury. Upon receipt of the tenth offered by the people, the Levites give a tenth to the priests. This is their rightful portion. The priests place the produce in Temple storerooms for later use. The chapter concludes with a summary statement of what the people, including the Levites, bind themselves to do. They vow to not neglect the House of God.

Remember It

Promises, promises. We all make them in our relationships. We promise to do, but sometimes we don't. This was the practice of some of the Jews, God's people. Some made vows to God to obey all that He commanded them to do, but while in captivity, they broke their promises. But we serve a merciful God of multiple chances. Under the leadership of Nehemiah, the people reestablished themselves as God's holy people. They renewed their vows and began anew to serve Him. God has made promises, too. He promises in Romans 8:39–40 that nothing can separate us from His love. So, when we repent because of our broken promises, He will open His arms and receive us again.

• • • • • • • • • • • • • • • • • •

Share It • Live It • Hear It

Invite your spouse, children, or family member to listen to Gospel music or religious hymns with you. Or listen with your class. Choose songs that honor God for His faithful love, goodness, and kindness. Read and reflect together on the lyrics of two songs.

In many ways, a covenant is the foundation of our church relationships. As members of the same Body, we should collectively honor God first, then we should honor one another by fulfilling a commitment to carry out the goals and purposes of the Church.

Take the opportunity to share with someone who needs to know about the challenges of perfectly following God's will. Then express the love of God so that the person does not feel that obedience to Him is hopeless.

@rhboydco

DDR

Devotional Readings for May 26–June 7, 2025

MONDAY	TUESDAY	WEDNESDAY	THURSDAY	FRIDAY	SATURDAY	SUNDAY
Honor God with Your First Fruits	Struggles of Faith	The Righteous Will Live by Faith	Half-hearted Giving	Give Your All	The Martyrs' Cry for Justice	Acceptable and Unacceptable Worship
Proverbs 3:1–10	Hebrews 10:26–34	Hebrews 10:35–11:4	Acts 5:1–11	Luke 20:45–21:4	Revelation 6:9–17	Genesis 4:1–15

GIFT–GIVING THAT MATTERS

BACKGROUND PASSAGE: GENESIS 4:1–25   **LESSON PASSAGE: GENESIS 4:1–15**

RESOURCES: *New National Baptist Hymnal 21st Century Edition,*
Boyd's Commentary for the Sunday School

KEY VERSE: And the Lord said unto Cain, Why art thou wroth? and why is thy countenance fallen? If thou doest well, shalt thou not be accepted? and if thou doest not well, sin lieth at the door. And unto thee shall be his desire, and thou shalt rule over him. (Genesis 4:6–7, KJV)

Intro

When asked, "What is the greatest gift you have received?" many people might tell of a piece a jewelry from a special person, or a much-needed vehicle for transportation, or even a simple gesture of kindness. All of these things are wonderful and will go a long way in creating delight in the heart and in daily life. But every person should consider the one gift that no one on this earth can give or should take away. It is the gift of life. This precious gift of life is only God's to give. In His omnipotence, God gave it to us when He spoke the world and its inhabitants into existence. Often in church, we hear someone say, "God woke me up this morning and started me on my way." This is a solidly true statement of God's love and power; for in His omnipotence, only God sustains every microorganism and every breath we take.

Without God's sovereign grace to keep us going, we would perish. It is God's breath that gives us life and God's breath that sustains that same life day-to-day, moment-by-moment. As Job said, "If he should take back his spirit to himself, and gather to himself his breath, all flesh would perish together, and man would return to dust" (Job 34:14–15). The gift of life God has given us should matter to every living person. Because of God's gift, we owe it to Him to live our lives given back to Him. In response, we realize our gifts we bring to God matter. This lesson helps us understand that there is a sacrifice that is pleasing to God.

Think About It

How does the way God gives and what He has given differ from the way you give and what you have offered in your life so far?

_____

_____

_____

_____

1. The Offerings of Cain and Abel (Genesis 4:1–5)

King James Version	NRSVue
AND Adam knew Eve his wife; and she conceived, and bare Cain, and said, I have gotten a man from the Lord.	NOW the man knew his wife Eve, and she conceived and bore Cain, saying, "I have produced a man with the help of the Lord."
2 And she again bare his brother Abel. And Abel was a keeper of sheep, but Cain was a tiller of the ground.	2 Next she bore his brother Abel. Now Abel was a keeper of sheep, and Cain a tiller of the ground.
3 And in process of time it came to pass, that Cain brought of the fruit of the ground an offering unto the Lord.	3 In the course of time Cain brought to the Lord an offering of the fruit of the ground,
4 And Abel, he also brought of the firstlings of his flock and of the fat thereof. And the Lord had respect unto Abel and to his offering:	4 and Abel for his part brought of the firstlings of his flock, their fat portions. And the Lord had regard for Abel and his offering,
5 But unto Cain and to his offering he had not respect. And Cain was very wroth, and his countenance fell.	5 but for Cain and his offering he had no regard. So Cain was very angry, and his countenance fell.

Know It

Following the sin of Adam and Eve in the Garden of Eden, they begin to fulfill God's original command to "be fruitful and multiply" (Gen. 1:28). Their firstborn son is named Cain, and soon after Eve births another son who is named Abel. Eve recognizes that she birthed her first son with the help of the Lord (v. 1). When Cain and Abel grew up, the boys chose different professions. Cain worked the ground, so he exhibited the skills of a farmer. He had the knowledge and foresight to plant seeds at a certain time. Cain also knew how to guard his crop from animals and keep weeds at bay. We can surmise Cain understood how to prepare the soil for each type of plant, provide nutrients and moisture, and develop ways to irrigate from rivers and streams. At that time, storage may have been difficult without a refrigerated environment. So, he more than likely had to create a way to retain sustenance. Cain indeed had agricultural skills.

Abel, however, was not a farmer; he was a shepherd. This vocation requires a different set of skills. Abel needed to guide his flock, keep them safe and prevent them from straying. He also needed to accept potential limitations of sheep. Sheep were weak and depended completely on the shepherd. We can surmise Abel skillfully using his staff to guide and correct the sheep, ensuring they were well feed, and determining the comfort needed so they could reproduce and increase in number.

As Cain and Abel grow up, they are expected to worship God with a sacrifice. Each brings to the Lord the product of his profession. This is long before the Hebrew sacrificial system set up by Moses. Perhaps the young men have learned the practice from their father, Adam. As a farmer, Cain brings some of his crops as a sacrificial gift to the Lord, probably spreading his produce before God in a dignified and beautiful way. But something is missing. By contrast, Abel's sacrificial gift consists of the firstborns of his flock, including fat portions. Later in their history, God's people would learn the firstfruits of our work belong to God.

The Lord looks with favor on Abel and his offering. But not so for Cain's offering (v. 5). The Bible does not mention the reason why Cain's offering is rejected. Some suggest their attitudes made a difference; others suggest a contrast between a generous and a miserly offering; still others speculate there was a difference in the quality of their offerings, and the Book of Hebrews speaks of the "better sacrifice" of Abel and that God "spoke well of his offerings" (Heb. 11:4). If the Lord declared that Cain's sacrifice was unacceptable, it is true. Cain's response to God's rejection is anger, but rather, should be a desire to correct what is unacceptable.

2. The Murder of Abel (Genesis 4:6–9)

King James Version	NRSVue
6 And the Lord said unto Cain, Why art thou wroth? and why is thy countenance fallen?	6 The Lord said to Cain, "Why are you angry, and why has your countenance fallen?
7 If thou doest well, shalt thou not be accepted? and if thou doest not well, sin lieth at the door. And unto thee shall be his desire, and thou shalt rule over him.	7 If you do well, will you not be accepted? And if you do not do well, sin is lurking at the door; its desire is for you, but you must master it."
8 And Cain talked with Abel his brother: and it came to pass, when they were in the field, that Cain rose up against Abel his brother, and slew him.	8 Cain said to his brother Abel, "Let us go out to the field." And when they were in the field, Cain rose up against his brother Abel, and killed him.
9 And the Lord said unto Cain, Where is Abel thy brother? And he said, I know not: Am I my brother's keeper?	9 Then the Lord said to Cain, "Where is your brother Abel?" He said, "I do not know; am I my brother's keeper?"

Cain had a poor attitude; he was angry and unwilling to accept God's decision on the offerings. Anger causes us to be someone we don't want to be. It robs us of kindness, love, and thoughtfulness. We should not allow this to happen in our relationships, especially with family. Anger can also distract us from what's important. We often ignore key facts—such as what emotion we are truly experiencing, the reasons behind it, and the reality that the person we are angry with is not angry with us. Additionally, Cain's actions show that unchecked anger leaves little to no room for reviewing events and situations with clarity or for seeking redirection. Cain's anger is directed toward God, who loves him deeply.

Even so, God turns to Cain in mercy and asks him questions that, if considered, can lead Cain to find understanding and repentance. Essentially, God asks Cain foundational questions regarding choice. He invites Cain to consider his actions regarding his choice of sacrifice and reminds Cain how easy it is to fall into sin, as well as to stand in acceptance. However, instead of confessing his sin and seeking to offer a better sacrifice, Cain allows sin to take over.

After sulking and letting anger have its way, Cain takes it out on his brother. In his next act, Cain must have determined that Abel had offered his first and last offering. In rage, Cain kills his brother. The hatred in Cain's heart could not find rest. So, he vented his rage on his brother. It was premeditated murder fueled by Cain's hatred. In verse 9, God asks, "Where is Abel your brother?" Of course, the all-knowing God knew Cain had murdered his brother. The Lord's question echoes His question to Cain's father after Adam and Eve eats forbidden fruit (Gen. 3:9). However instead of being truthful, Cain offers a snide response: "I do not know; am I my brother's keeper?" (v. 9). This infamous question does not win Cain favor with God.

3. The Punishment of Cain (Genesis 4:10–15)

King James Version	New Revised Standard Version
10 And he said, What hast thou done? the voice of thy brother's blood crieth unto me from the ground.	**10** And the Lord said, "What have you done? Listen; your brother's blood is crying out to me from the ground!
11 And now art thou cursed from the earth, which hath opened her mouth to receive thy brother's blood from thy hand;	**11** And now you are cursed from the ground, which has opened its mouth to receive your brother's blood from your hand.
12 When thou tillest the ground, it shall not henceforth yield unto thee her strength; a fugitive and a vagabond shalt thou be in the earth.	**12** When you till the ground, it will no longer yield to you its strength; you will be a fugitive and a wanderer on the earth."
13 And Cain said unto the Lord, My punishment is greater than I can bear.	**13** Cain said to the Lord, "My punishment is greater than I can bear!

3. The Punishment of Cain (Genesis 4:10–15)

King James Version	NRSVue
14 Behold, thou hast driven me out this day from the face of the earth; and from thy face shall I be hid; and I shall be a fugitive and a vagabond in the earth; and it shall come to pass, that every one that findeth me shall slay me. **15** And the Lord said unto him, Therefore whosoever slayeth Cain, vengeance shall be taken on him sevenfold. And the Lord set a mark upon Cain, lest any finding him should kill him.	**14** Today you have driven me away from the soil, and I shall be hidden from your face; I shall be a fugitive and a wanderer on the earth, and anyone who meets me may kill me." **15** Then the Lord said to him, "Not so! Whoever kills Cain will suffer a sevenfold vengeance." And the Lord put a mark on Cain, so that no one who came upon him would kill him.

The biblical narrative says we will be held accountable for our attitude (see e.g. Matt. 12:36–37; Rom. 14:12). God holds Cain responsible for the hateful attitude that causes him to murder his brother. But before any punishment is announced, God once again gives Cain opportunity to confess and repent. God asks, "What have you done?" (v. 10). This question gives Cain yet another opportunity to confess what he has done. But in his silence, Cain refuses. Ultimately, a heart that is angry reflects sin. We may think there's no way we would ever get angry enough to kill someone. But Jesus says anger and murder are the same. In Matthew 5:21–22, He clarifies that we sin when we become angry enough to murder. That is, we have already committed murder in our hearts when rage becomes our guide.

God pronounces Cain's punishment (vv. 11–12). Though Abel never speaks, his blood cries out from the ground. God's punishment begins with a curse. He tells Cain that he is more cursed than the ground. He would be separated from the ground because he polluted it with the innocent blood of Abel. This means the farmer Cain would no longer enjoy the fruit of the ground. In an instant, his occupation is no more. This curse destroys his life and causes Cain to be a "fugitive and a wanderer"(v. 14).

Cain responds to God's discipline with self–pity, stating his punishment is more than he can bear (v. 13). Cain is afraid he will be hunted and eventually murdered. Thereby, God tempers His judgment with mercy by placing a mark on Cain in order to preserve his life (v. 15). This is God's grace in action. The Apostle John said Cain killed Abel because Cain's actions were evil and Abel's actions were righteous (1 John 3:12). Abel offered God a gift that mattered. It reflected that his heart and his attitude was pleasing to God. This was true and proper worship—gift-giving that mattered.

Remember It

Both Cain and Abel made sacrificial gifts to God, but Cain's gift was rejected. Cain became angry. Another word to describe his attitude is "furious." In the original Hebrew, this means to "become kindled with intensity, to rise in emotion like fire." Cain's response to God's rejection gives a clue that his attitude may have been wrong from the start. God knows the heart. Even so, we learn from Cain the need for a contrite spirit that can grow in our capacity to receive correction. Cain's lack thereof—his kindling anger—ended in the murder of his brother. Sometimes, like Cain, we choose what we should not. When this happens, we are encouraged to ask God for help and receive His mercy.

• • • • • • • • • • • • • • • • • • •

Share It • Live It • Hear It

Songs can serve multiple purposes. Two of which are to soothe us when we are upset or angry and to be an offertory gift to God. Find three songs in both categories and create a playlist. The next time you are angry, listen to or recite the lyrics as a means of correction and a praise offering to God.

Abel's offering didn't take anything away from Cain. But it evoked unwarranted anger. We should be careful how we respond when others do well. Write and memorize a prayer of confession to use when comparison taints your gift-giving to God.

Encourage fellow believers to give God their best. This includes not only our tithes, but the things we do at work, in church, and in our homes. Encourage others in their gift-giving with affirmations and the example of proper attitudes toward one another.

ⓧ ⊙ ⓕ

@rhboydco

Devotional Readings for June 2–8, 2025

DDR

	MONDAY	TUESDAY	WEDNESDAY	THURSDAY	FRIDAY	SATURDAY	SUNDAY
	Obedience to God's Command	Jesus Joins Us in the Storm	Peace through the Word	God Protects	A Herald of Righteousness	A Cry for Deliverance	A Covenant of Peace
	Genesis 6:11–22	John 6:15–20	John 1 4:18–27	Genesis 7:11–24	2 Peter 2:1–9	Psalm 77:1–2, 7–19	Genesis 8:13–22; 9:11–13

THE RAINBOW PROMISE

BACKGROUND PASSAGE: GENESIS 6:1–9:17
PRINT PASSAGE: GENESIS 8:13–22; 9:11–13

RESOURCES: *New National Baptist Hymnal 21st Century Edition,*
Boyd's Commentary for the Sunday School

KEY VERSE: [God said,] "I have set my bow in the clouds, and it shall be a sign of the covenant between me and the earth." (Genesis 9:13, NRSVue)

Intro

Hurricane Helene, one of the most devastating storms in U.S. history, struck in September 2024. It caused widespread destruction to a large area of the Southeastern portion of our country. Millions of people lost power for days, some for weeks. Many businesses shut down because of damage to building structures. A Florida pipeline that provided fuel to jet planes was damaged. Georgia's poultry farms were damaged. Other states that Helene touched, including Tennessee, Virginia, South Carolina, and North Carolina, sustained significant damage. The combined impact on human life totaled more than 230 killed and at least forty-one missing.

The most impactful element of Helene was the widespread flooding. Rainfall totals exceeded ten inches over a period of four days. This record rainfall caused rivers to overflow and produced flash flooding, road washouts, and even landslides in some areas. Many people lost their homes and businesses, which contained precious family possessions. During the aftermath of the storm, they stood amid rubble and debris which was once their home.

However, the tragedy of Hurricane Helene, in contrast to the biblical flood, did not stop people from moving forward. When Noah stepped out of the ark, all life, including plants, animals, fish, and humans were gone. But God did not abandon humanity. He used a rainbow as a symbol of His promise to never destroy people again. The rainbow is a symbol of God's love.

Think About It

The terms of The Noahic covenant includes a rainbow promise. What does this covenant help us understand about the nature of God, including God's love?

_____

_____

_____

_____

1. The End of the Flood (Genesis 8:13–14)

King James Version	NRSVue
AND it came to pass in the six hundredth and first year, in the first month, the first day of the month, the waters were dried up from off the earth: and Noah removed the covering of the ark, and looked, and, behold, the face of the ground was dry.	IN the six hundred first year, in the first month, on the first day of the month, the waters were dried up from the earth; and Noah removed the covering of the ark, and looked, and saw that the face of the ground was drying.
14 And in the second month, on the seven and twentieth day of the month, was the earth dried.	**14** In the second month, on the twenty-seventh day of the month, the earth was dry.

Know It

The events of the flood make up an epic story—so much so that it has been retold repeatedly in books and movies, in various ways. Also, a life–sized Noah's Ark has been erected as a museum called *Ark Encounter*. This extensive narrative in the book of Genesis describes how God judged the sinfulness of humankind. Because wickedness had spread all over the earth, God regretted He had made people, and with grief in His heart, God decided to wipe them off the face of the earth (Gen. 6:6–7). Hence, the reason for the flood. But there was one man that pleased God. His name was Noah. Noah was the only follower of God left in his generation.

Noah has to be a man of patience, and the Bible describes Noah as a person of obedience who did everything just as God commanded him (Gen. 6:22). This was said of him at several different points as he followed God. One of the things Noah is commanded to do is build an ark, a large boat, to God's specifications. And though Noah was not a skilled shipbuilder, when he finishes, the ark is sea–worthy and ready to be inhabited. God commands Noah to take his wife, their sons, and their sons' wives and go into the ark. He is commanded to take with him a female and male of every kind of animal and bird on the earth. Noah is six–hundred years old when the earth is flooded (Gen. 7:6).

The rains fall for forty days and forty nights (Gen. 7:4). Then Noah uses birds to methodically determine when it is safe enough for his family to leave the ark. First, he releases a raven, which flies around the ark until the water dries up. Then he releases a dove, which, in contrast to the raven, returns to Noah because it cannot find a place to perch, indicating that water still covers the surface of the earth. The second dove Noah sends out returns with a freshly plucked olive leaf. This tells Noah the water has receded from the earth enough for plants to grow. Finally, the third dove released never returns. This indicates the earth is dry enough for the bird to survive on its own and, therefore, so can humans.

2. The New Start (Genesis 8:15–22)

King James Version	NRSVue
15 And God spake unto Noah, saying,	**15** Then God said to Noah,
16 Go forth of the ark, thou, and thy wife, and thy sons, and thy sons' wives with thee.	**16** "Go out of the ark, you and your wife, and your sons and your sons' wives with you.
17 Bring forth with thee every living thing that is with thee, of all flesh, both of fowl, and of cattle, and of every creeping thing that creepeth upon the earth; that they may breed abundantly in the earth, and be fruitful, and multiply upon the earth.	**17** Bring out with you every living thing that is with you of all flesh—birds and animals and every creeping thing that creeps on the earth—so that they may abound on the earth, and be fruitful and multiply on the earth."
18 And Noah went forth, and his sons, and his wife, and his sons' wives with him:	**18** So Noah went out with his sons and his wife and his sons' wives.
19 Every beast, every creeping thing, and every fowl, and whatsoever creepeth upon the earth, after their kinds, went forth out of the ark.	**19** And every animal, every creeping thing, and every bird, everything that moves on the earth, went out of the ark by families.
20 And Noah builded an altar unto the Lord; and took of every clean beast, and of every clean fowl, and offered burnt offerings on the altar.	**20** Then Noah built an altar to the Lord, and took of every clean animal and of every clean bird, and offered burnt offerings on the altar.
21 And the Lord smelled a sweet savour; and the Lord said in his heart, I will not again curse the ground any more for man's sake; for the imagination of man's heart is evil from his youth; neither will I again smite any more every thing living, as I have done.	**21** And when the Lord smelled the pleasing odor, the Lord said in his heart, "I will never again curse the ground because of humankind, for the inclination of the human heart is evil from youth; nor will I ever again destroy every living creature as I have done.
22 While the earth remaineth, seedtime and harvest, and cold and heat, and summer and winter, and day and night shall not cease.	**22** As long as the earth endures, seedtime and harvest, cold and heat, summer and winter, day and night, shall not cease."

Even though the earth is dry, Noah waits for God to command him to come out of the ark. Noah did not want to get ahead of God when he had done so well throughout the course of the flood. For more than a year, Noah had patiently done all that God had commanded him to do (Gen. 8:13). Noah and his family were sheltered in the ark all that time. One can only imagine whether they experienced the walls closing in on them or whether they found something interesting to do as time passed. There was always the work of caring for the animals and birds, which must have been a massive undertaking. They had to also care for themselves—bathing and eating was probably resolved first. When the third dove did not return, we don't know if Noah and his family were excited at the possibility of leaving the ark, or afraid.

Subsequently, God commands Noah to come out of the ark. Further, God tells Noah to bring his whole family out with him as well as all the living creatures. It was time for a new start—time to begin life again. God wants His creation to be fruitful and multiply (Gen. 1:26–28). The preflood culture focused on wickedness and fleshly pleasures. But procreation in a righteous environment honors God with new life. Noah and all who were in the ark with him would restore what was lost.

There must have been overwhelming emotions expressed as Noah and his family first set foot on sturdy and steady dry land. No longer would they be tossed about by the rolling waters of the flood. Immediately, Noah gives honor to God by building an altar, humbly worshiping the God who saw them through a devastating, catastrophic event. They may have been struck by the reality of this when they looked around to see that they had survived only by God's mercy and grace. The earth was empty of everything but them.

Verse 21 notes that God smells the aroma of Noah's offering. We know God does not have a human body like ours, so He does not have a nose for smelling. When a human characteristic is applied to God, it is called an *anthropomorphism*. That God smells the pleasing aroma is a figurative way to say that the Lord took notice of Noah's sacrifice, and it pleased Him. Some of the clean animals on the ark were used by Noah as a sacrifice to God. We should be challenged to live our lives so that God will notice our total commitment to Him.

As a result of Noah's demonstration of gratitude and commitment, God says in His heart He will never again curse the ground because of the wickedness of humanity (v. 21). He vows to Himself that He will never again destroy all living creatures. Despite the sinful nature of people, God's grace and love will prevail.

3. The Sign of the Rainbow (Genesis 9:11–13)

King James Version	NRSVue
11 And I will establish my covenant with you, neither shall all flesh be cut off any more by the waters of a flood; neither shall there any more be a flood to destroy the earth.	**11** I establish my covenant with you, that never again shall all flesh be cut off by the waters of a flood, and never again shall there be a flood to destroy the earth."
12 And God said, This is the token of the covenant which I make between me and you and every living creature that is with you, for perpetual generations:	**12** God said, "This is the sign of the covenant that I make between me and you and every living creature that is with you, for all future generations:
13 I do set my bow in the cloud, and it shall be for a token of a covenant between me and the earth.	**13** I have set my bow in the clouds, and it shall be a sign of the covenant between me and the earth.

God places the words He spoke to Himself in a covenant with Noah, commonly referred to as "The Noahic Covenant" in theological circles. The Noahic Covenant ensures that humanity will survive. It is God, Elohim, who with great power created the earth and all its inhabitants; and it is God who, by that same power, can destroy it. But God pledges that He will preserve what He has made and allow the people and the earth He created to flourish.

There was nothing Noah needed to do. Only God is obligated to keep His promise. It is a promise that is made between the sovereign Lord and Noah, his descendants, and every living creature on the earth. It is a promise no human can break or amend. A view of history allows us to see that this covenant provides the platform on which Christ would enter the world. Moreover, this covenant reveals God's love for all that He has made. Because God promises to never again destroy the inhabitants of the world, one day there will be a new earth. Because of this promise we know God will indeed never leave us or forsake us.

God institutes a sign of His covenant with Noah. This sign is not for God, but for Noah—for us. The sign is the rainbow that forms in the clouds. The rainbow is a weather phenomenon that appears during and after rain. They usually appear as full circles, but only the arc is visible. Some people have used the rainbow as a symbol of non–biblical social movements. It has also been used to represent a nation's philosophy and political alliances as well as business and product logos. But the rainbow is God's creation. It is first and foremost a visible representation of God's commitment to us. May we never lose the wonder we naturally feel when a rainbow appears after a storm. It is a God–ordained symbol of His love and faithfulness. The attempt by humanity to change its godly representation does not take away the beauty and wholesomeness of what God has made.

Remember It

God gave humanity a chance at a new start by destroying all that was evil and corrupt and restarting with a blameless, righteous man. This man was named Noah. Noah was a man of great patience and obedience toward God. God caused a great flood to cover the earth for forty days and forty nights. When the storm was over, Noah emerged from the ark that kept him, his family, and all the living creators safe. His first act was to worship God who demonstrated His awesome power and His faithful love through this event. God responded with a rainbow that symbolized this renewed commitment to humanity. We can live at peace knowing that God will never again destroy the people of the earth with a flood.

• • • • • • • • • • • • • • • • • • • •

Share It • Live It • Hear It

After the flood, Noah made a new start by worshiping God. What would your song honoring new life sound like? Worship God with a new song that has been created in your heart by the Holy Spirit.

Noah had no idea what awaited him when he opened the door and emerged from the ark. He and his family had just gone through a catastrophic event that no other person survived. The only thing Noah was certain of was that God was with Him. We can rest assured that no matter the storm, when God is with you, there's a rainbow waiting.

The next time you see a rainbow, share with someone that it is a reminder of God's love, which He demonstrated when His Son, Jesus, died and rose again to redeem every person on earth.

Get Social
Start an online conversation about **#COMMITMENT**. Share your views and tag us @rhboydco and use #rhboydco.

@rhboydco

DDR

Devotional Readings for June 9–15, 2025

	MONDAY	TUESDAY	WEDNESDAY	THURSDAY	FRIDAY	SATURDAY	SUNDAY
	God Promises a Son	Abraham's Righteous Faith	Life Out of Death	A Blessing to the Nations	Joy for Weeping	Abraham's Courageous Faith	God Will Provide a Lamb
	Genesis 17:15–22	Romans 4:1–15	Romans 4:16–25	Genesis 12:1–7	Psalms 125–126	Hebrews 11:8–12	Genesis 22:1–14

ULTIMATE ALLEGIANCE

BACKGROUND PASSAGE: GENESIS 22:1–19   **PRINT PASSAGE: GENESIS 22:1–14**

RESOURCES: *New National Baptist Hymnal 21st Century Edition,*
Boyd's Commentary for the Sunday School

KEY VERSE: And Abraham called the name of that place Jehovahjireh: as it is said to this day, In the mount of the Lord it shall be seen. (Genesis 22:14, KJV)

Intro

Mt. Everest, the world's highest peak, has been the focus of mountaineers and curiosity-seekers alike. These individuals are amongst those who have endeavored to reach the top of the mountain. This dangerous and strenuous hike has tested the limits of thousands of climbers trying to reach the top. As of 2024, an estimated 340 have died undertaking this effort. In 2003, Sibusiso Vilane from South Africa became the first Black climber to reach the top. Summiteers find the Mt. Everest climb grueling because of sub-freezing temperatures, slippery slopes, strong winds, and blackouts. With a rock height of 29,031.69 feet (8,848.86 meters) above sea level, which is about 5.5 miles (8.8 kilometers) tall, climbers brave enough to attempt the summit will be tested physically, emotionally, and mentally with every step.

In the same way, some of life's situations can test our limits. Think about the effort it takes to raise children, maintain a household budget, navigate careers, and reconcile relationships that have gone sour. In 2024, politics seemed to bring out the worst in people who placed their values above respect for others. Life will always test us; we can't escape it. The testing of our lives also includes the testing for our faith. God wants us to develop deep faith so that our trust in Him is strong. Today's lesson about Abraham and Isaac helps us understand what it takes to stay the course when spiritual tests seem to surpass our limits.

Think About It

What difference does it make in our lives to abide by strong biblical principles and values that support a firm faith and confidence in God?

_____

_____

_____

_____

1. Tests Will Happen (Genesis 22:1–2)

King James Version	NRSVue
AND it came to pass after these things, that God did tempt Abraham, and said unto him, Abraham: and he said, Behold, here I am.	AFTER these things God tested Abraham. He said to him, "Abraham!" And he said, "Here I am."
2 And he said, Take now thy son, thine only son Isaac, whom thou lovest, and get thee into the land of Moriah; and offer him there for a burnt offering upon one of the mountains which I will tell thee of.	**2** He said, "Take your son, your only son Isaac, whom you love, and go to the land of Moriah, and offer him there as a burnt offering on one of the mountains that I shall show you."

Know It

God chose Abraham to be the father of nations because of Abraham's commitment to Him. Being called to be the patriarch of every person on earth ultimately invites Abraham to demonstrate a higher level of spirituality. Abraham, like us, needed to consistently grow spiritually. Biblically speaking, growth requires testing. It is a crucial part of the Christian life because it teaches us to fully rely on who God is and what He can do. The beginning of this narrative provides a warning on what was about to happen; Abraham's faith in God's absolute righteous judgment was to be put on the line.

God gives Abraham what seems to be incredibly outlandish instructions. He asks Abraham, who was well over a century old, to sacrifice his "only son." Abraham is to take the very son the Lord has promised him for twenty-five years to the land of Moriah and offer him as a sacrifice. Human sacrifices, common in ancient paganism, was wrong for the righteous people of God. But here God's command takes precedence over human customs. God will often put us to the test by requesting what seems extreme to us. God might instruct us to forgive someone who has hurt us, move to a new location, or spend time in a difficult ministry. Many times, we wrestle with such requests because they seem nonsensical and beyond our limits. We should remember God's love when we are tested, because no difficult test that God brings our way is intended to hurt or demean us, but rather to increase our trust in Him. Consider the work of a personal trainer who often increases the weight over time. This increase is meant to build muscle. Even though God's testing may be difficult, it is meant to bring the best out of us.

Some Bible interpreters believe that God tempted Abraham. But test and tempt are two different words. *Tempt* means to entice someone to do something, while *test* means to prove the quality of someone. The Bible reads that God will never tempt us (James 1:13–14). Satan *tempts* us to sin to create a wall between God and us, but God *tests* us to build us up and pull us closer to Him.

2. God Will Guide Us (Genesis 22:3–10)

King James Version	NRSVue
3 And Abraham rose up early in the morning, and saddled his ass, and took two of his young men with him, and Isaac his son, and clave the wood for the burnt offering, and rose up, and went unto the place of which God had told him.	**3** So Abraham rose early in the morning, saddled his donkey, and took two of his young men with him, and his son Isaac; he cut the wood for the burnt offering, and set out and went to the place in the distance that God had shown him.
4 Then on the third day Abraham lifted up his eyes, and saw the place afar off.	**4** On the third day Abraham looked up and saw the place far away.
5 And Abraham said unto his young men, Abide ye here with the ass; and I and the lad will go yonder and worship, and come again to you.	**5** Then Abraham said to his young men, "Stay here with the donkey; the boy and I will go over there; we will worship, and then we will come back to you."
6 And Abraham took the wood of the burnt offering, and laid it upon Isaac his son; and he took the fire in his hand, and a knife; and they went both of them together.	**6** Abraham took the wood of the burnt offering and laid it on his son Isaac, and he himself carried the fire and the knife. So the two of them walked on together.
7 And Isaac spake unto Abraham his father, and said, My father: and he said, Here am I, my son. And he said, Behold the fire and the wood: but where is the lamb for a burnt offering?	**7** Isaac said to his father Abraham, "Father!" And he said, "Here I am, my son." He said, "The fire and the wood are here, but where is the lamb for a burnt offering?"
8 And Abraham said, My son, God will provide himself a lamb for a burnt offering: so they went both of them together.	**8** Abraham said, "God himself will provide the lamb for a burnt offering, my son." So the two of them walked on together.
9 And they came to the place which God had told him of; and Abraham built an altar there, and laid the wood in order, and bound Isaac his son, and laid him on the altar upon the wood.	**9** When they came to the place that God had shown him, Abraham built an altar there and laid the wood in order. He bound his son Isaac, and laid him on the altar, on top of the wood.
10 And Abraham stretched forth his hand, and took the knife to slay his son.	**10** Then Abraham reached out his hand and took the knife to kill his son.

God and Abraham have a lot of history between them, and God had brought Abraham to a place of great trust. Abraham continues moving forward, even though he could choose to quit at any point—whether while preparing the wood, saddling his donkey, or building the altar. There is no evidence that Abraham knew God would provide a different kind of sacrifice and Isaac would be unharmed. Maybe Abraham considered "that God was able to raise [Isaac] up, even from the dead" (Heb. 11:19, KJV). This journey is also a test for Isaac, who assists his aged father. As Isaac trusts his earthly father, he surely also trusts his heavenly Father. Sometimes, we refuse God's guidance because we don't understand it, but that is making ourselves equal with God (see e.g. Isa. 55:8–9).

3. God Will Provide (Genesis 22:11–14)

King James Version	NRSVue
11 And the angel of the Lord called unto him out of heaven, and said, Abraham, Abraham: and he said, Here am I.	**11** But the angel of the Lord called to him from heaven, and said, "Abraham, Abraham!" And he said, "Here I am."
12 And he said, Lay not thine hand upon the lad, neither do thou any thing unto him: for now I know that thou fearest God, seeing thou hast not withheld thy son, thine only son from me.	**12** He said, "Do not lay your hand on the boy or do anything to him; for now I know that you fear God, since you have not withheld your son, your only son, from me."
13 And Abraham lifted up his eyes, and looked, and behold behind him a ram caught in a thicket by his horns: and Abraham went and took the ram, and offered him up for a burnt offering in the stead of his son.	**13** And Abraham looked up and saw a ram, caught in a thicket by its horns. Abraham went and took the ram and offered it up as a burnt offering instead of his son.
14 And Abraham called the name of that place Jehovahjireh: as it is said to this day, In the mount of the Lord it shall be seen. After these things God tested Abraham. He said to him, "Abraham!" And he said, "Here I am."	**14** So Abraham called that place "The Lord will provide"; as it is said to this day, "On the mount of the Lord it shall be provided."

At any point in this awful journey, God could have stopped Abraham and said, "It is enough. I see your faith. You have passed the test." But God does not. God allows Abraham to go through the entire ritual sacrifice. Only when Abraham reaches out his hand and takes the knife to slay his son does God stop him. The Angel of the Lord calls Abraham by name, and exactly as he did in verse 1, Abraham says, "Here I am." At this, the angel reveals the details of the test Abraham had faced.

Picture Abraham's response at this news. He must have dropped the knife and, overwhelmed with emotion, fell to his knees and worshiped God. This had to be a worshipful moment for Isaac as well; one that solidified his own faith in God. Isaac escaped death because God provides a ram that Abraham sacrifices as a burnt offering instead of his son. That day, both Abraham and Isaac experience the truth that God will provide. Abraham fittingly calls the place "Jehovah Jireh"—meaning "the Lord will provide" (v. 14).

Remember It

A test was all it took for Abraham to trust God more earnestly and fully. It was a test in which he was asked to give up something he valued more than anything—something promised to him that had taken what probably seemed like an eternity to materialize. Abraham was challenged to sacrifice his son as an offering but was ultimately called to trust God at His word. Similarly, God asks His people to trust and obey Him completely. In our walk with God, we are challenged to surrender all that we own, including life itself if necessary. Just as Abraham trusted God to find a way to save a life that he loved, we must stand strong in faith that God is able to provide what we need at the right time.

• • • • • • • • • • • • • • • • • • •

Share It • Live It • Hear It

Find and play the instrumental version of a worship song while reflectively reading through Genesis 22:1–14. Ask the Holy Spirit to open your heart to grow deeper in understanding God's desire for us to fully trust Him.

How do we stay the course when spiritual tests seem to surpass our limits? God's Word encourages us to walk with God daily through Bible study, prayer, and worship. We also have the tools of fasting and fellowship. Like Abraham, the longer we walk with God, the stronger our faith will become.

Almost everyone knows the story of Abraham and Isaac. When you have a divine encounter, share Abraham's willingness to sacrifice his son Isaac. Then, discuss how God similarly allowed His Son to be sacrificed for us.

Get Social
Start an online conversation about **#PROVISION**.
Share your views and tag us @rhboydco and use #rhboydco.

@rhboydco

DDR

Devotional Readings for June 16–22, 2025

	MONDAY	TUESDAY	WEDNESDAY	THURSDAY	FRIDAY	SATURDAY	SUNDAY
	Love the Alien as Yourself	Isaac's Prayer for Rebekah	Living as an Alien	God Will Supply Every Need	God Blesses and Provides	Live in Harmony; Welcome One Another	Making Peace with Others
	Leviticus 19:30–37	Genesis 25:19–28	Genesis 26:1–11	Philippians 4:10–19	Genesis 26:12–23	Romans 15:1–13	Genesis 26:24–33

DIGGING YOUR OWN WELL

BACKGROUND PASSAGE: GENESIS 26:1–33　　**PRINT PASSAGE: GENESIS 26:24–33**

RESOURCES: *New National Baptist Hymnal 21st Century Edition,*
Boyd's Commentary for the Sunday School

> **KEY VERSE:** [Isaac] built an altar there, called on the name of the LORD, and pitched his tent there. And there Isaac's servants dug a well. (Genesis 26:25, NRSVue)

Intro

Pharrell Williams, the popular R&B singer and songwriter, is best known for his megahit "Happy," a song that nearly everyone loves to sing and dance along to. Pharrell grew up in Virginia. While appearing as a guest on a 2021 episode of the PBS television show, "Finding Your Roots," with Dr. Henry Louis Gates, he discovered an ancestry that is less than happy. Pharrell's traceable family story began with his great-great-grandfather, a man named Fenner Williams.

Grandpa Fenner had a sister named Jane Arrington, who participated in the government-sponsored Slave Narrative Project late in the 1930s. To ready herself for the interview, she wrote down her personal experiences with enslavement. Through her notes, Pharrell learned that Grandpa Fenner had been enslaved for the first ten years of his life. She shared details of their daily lives on a cotton plantation, revealing the degradation they endured each day.

Pharrell responded to the revelation with mixed emotions of grief and anger. Though most African Americans' ancestry includes similar stories, Pharrell was able to read about it firsthand from his aunt. Unlike Isaac, who had an ancestry full of faith and favor, Pharrell had an ancestry full of intense hatred and abuse. Even with favor, however, Isaac had to make his own way. Like Isaac, Pharrell made his own way with the life that was handed to him. In a sense, Pharrell dug his own well and became a renowned music maker, bringing joy to the world.

Think About It

What prevents most believers from "digging our own well," and how can placing God at the center of our lives help us to turn our lives around?

_____

_____

_____

_____

1. Isaac Finds a Home (Genesis 26:24–25)

King James Version	NRSVue
And the Lord appeared unto him the same night, and said, I am the God of Abraham thy father: fear not, for I am with thee, and will bless thee, and multiply thy seed for my servant Abraham's sake.	**And** that very night the Lord appeared to him and said, "I am the God of your father Abraham; do not be afraid, for I am with you and will bless you and make your offspring numerous for my servant Abraham's sake."
25 And he builded an altar there, and called upon the name of the Lord, and pitched his tent there: and there Isaac's servants digged a well.	**25** So he built an altar there, called on the name of the Lord, and pitched his tent there. And there Isaac's servants dug a well.

Know It

Isaac, the promised son of Abraham, begins to build on the legacy of his father. Isaac inherits everything from Abraham, including God's promise to make his descendants a great nation (Gen. 25:5). Throughout his life, Isaac follows God, allowing God to guide him. Following the death of Abraham, Isaac and his wife settle in Beer Lahai Roi (Gen. 25:11). At the start of chapter 26 there is a famine in the land. Because of the famine, Isaac goes to Abimelech who, at that time, is the king of the Philistines in Gerar. This is an early encounter with a nation that would become arch-enemies of God's people. The king gives Isaac permission to stay in the land. It's not long, however, before Abimelech asks Isaac to move away because Isaac grows increasingly wealthy (vv. 12–16).

The Philistines are so envious of Isaac that they sabotage Isaac's wells by filling them with dirt (v. 14). When Isaac moves to another well, he faces more opposition from the Philistines, and the same thing happens twice (vv. 17–20). Isaac persists, and he and his men dig yet another well—this time, without opposition (v. 22). This third well is clearly where God wants Isaac to settle. That night, the Lord speaks to Isaac. God reminds Isaac who He is, assures Isaac he need not be afraid, and retells of his promised, ancestral blessings. God makes a historical connection from Abraham to Isaac. This helps us trust that no matter what we face, God is a God of generations. What He promises will come to pass.

Isaac's response to God is to build an altar, worship, and settle down (v. 25). Isaac recognizes this space as the place where God wants him to be. Further, Isaac knows the customs of the land. He recognizes that he can continue to live in the area only if people are working and there is a well that provides water. This is demonstrated by the number of times Isaac moves when he is confronted by the Philistines over his wells. Wells were vital to life in Isaac's day; people and their flocks needed water to thrive. Isaac's persistence to dig his own well makes it clear that he has found a home and intends to remain in the land.

2. Isaac Resolves a Relationship (Genesis 26:26–29)

King James Version	NRSVue
26 Then Abimelech went to him from Gerar, and Ahuzzath one of his friends, and Phichol the chief captain of his army.	26 Then Abimelech went to him from Gerar, with Ahuzzath his adviser and Phicol the commander of his army.
27 And Isaac said unto them, Wherefore come ye to me, seeing ye hate me, and have sent me away from you?	27 Isaac said to them, "Why have you come to me, seeing that you hate me and have sent me away from you?"
28 And they said, We saw certainly that the Lord was with thee: and we said, Let there be now an oath betwixt us, even betwixt us and thee, and let us make a covenant with thee;	28 They said, "We see plainly that the Lord has been with you; so we say, let there be an oath between you and us, and let us make a covenant with you
29 That thou wilt do us no hurt, as we have not touched thee, and as we have done unto thee nothing but good, and have sent thee away in peace: thou art now the blessed of the Lord.	29 so that you will do us no harm, just as we have not touched you and have done to you nothing but good and have sent you away in peace. You are now the blessed of the Lord."

Back in Gerar, Abimelech still does not seem to be satisfied with Isaac's presence or with what Isaac is doing. No matter what Abimelech and the Philistines did, Isaac still seemed to prosper and be successful. This may have caused Abimelech to feel threatened by Isaac, who still lived nearby and held so much power. Therefore, Abimelech changes his strategy and decides to pay a visit to Isaac. He brings Ahuzzath, his personal adviser, and Phicol, the commander of his army, along with him.

This meeting has all the workings of a peace talk. But Isaac knows better and addresses them with caution. After the quarrels over the wells, it makes sense. Isaac asks pointedly, "Why have you come to me, seeing that you hate me and have sent me away from you?" (v. 27). With this question, Isaac elicits explanation from the men. This helps to clear the air so the discussion can move forward. Abimelech and his men acknowledge God's presence with Isaac, realizing that despite their actions—such as vandalizing his wells—this steadfast man of God continues to prosper. This means it would be to their advantage to make Isaac a friend rather than an enemy. This seems to be a repeat of what happened between the first Abimelech and Abraham in chapter 21.

We might say Abimelech's response to Isaac reveals an "if you can't beat them, join them" kind of approach. The Philistines obviously realize that what they are attempting to fight in Isaac is something beyond Isaac. They opposed a power greater than Isaac alone. As a result, they ask that an agreement, or covenant, be made between them and Isaac. The Philistines voice the terms of the agreement, asking for a treaty that Isaac and his divine help would not harm them. To ensure that Isaac agrees, they remind Isaac of the goodwill they extended to him when they first met as well as when they asked Isaac to leave. The Philistines contend that they had not harmed Isaac or Rebekah when the opportunity was theirs to do so.

3. Isaac Makes a Covenant (Genesis 26:30–33)

King James Version	NRSVue
30 And he made them a feast, and they did eat and drink.	**30** So he made them a feast, and they ate and drank.
31 And they rose up betimes in the morning, and sware one to another: and Isaac sent them away, and they departed from him in peace.	**31** In the morning they rose early and exchanged oaths; and Isaac set them on their way, and they departed from him in peace.
32 And it came to pass the same day, that Isaac's servants came, and told him concerning the well which they had digged, and said unto him, We have found water.	**32** That same day Isaac's servants came and told him about the well that they had dug, and said to him, "We have found water!"
33 And he called it Shebah: therefore the name of the city is Beersheba unto this day.	**33** He called it Shibah; therefore the name of the city is Beer-sheba to this day.

NOTES:

Isaac's immediate response to the resolved relationship is a feast, even though no agreement had been made yet. That the two parties share a meal could mean that Isaac was in agreement with the offered terms of the agreement. Providing this meal also insinuates that Isaac is in charge. But Abimelech and his party would have to wait until morning to find out what was going to happen.

The next morning, Isaac agrees to the terms. Both parties swear an oath that they will abide by the agreement. Then, Isaac sends them on their way in peace. Surely, Isaac can see God is working. From the famine and his encounter with Abimelech to the quarrels over the wells, the digging of his own well, and the agreement with Abimelech, Isaac can clearly see the mighty hand of God at work in his life. That same day, Isaac's servants come to him and share they have found water! This discovery is further confirmation of God's grace extended to Isaac. Isaac could now rest comfortably in the land, with peaceful neighbors and provisions sustained by water.

Remember It

Isaac, the promised son of Abraham, inherited the blessings of God. Isaac had been raised to follow God; as God guided Abraham, He also would guide Isaac. The privilege of a strong, godly ancestry and legacy belonged to Isaac. So, when Isaac sought a place of safety for him and his family, God led Isaac to find that place by moving him from one well to another. Eventually, Isaac had to dig his own well and that is where God settled him. Sometimes, when seeking our place in life, persistence against opposition may be required before things settle. God invites us to open our hearts and discern where He is leading us to dig our own well. Remember: what God says goes; His promises always materialize.

● ● ● ● ● ● ● ● ● ● ● ● ● ● ● ● ● ● ●

Share It • Live It • Hear It

Listen to the song "Lead Me, Guide Me," by Velma Willis on YouTube or another music platform. Reflect on your ancestry and how God has led you to dig your own well. Consider how God is both a God of generations and of gaps.

Get Social
Start an online conversation about **#PERSISTENCE**.
Share your views and tag us @rhboydco and use #rhboydco.

Despite our ancestry, God has a life that is planned for each of us. Spend time in prayer, asking God to confirm that you are living according to His will. If not, invite Him, through His Holy Spirit, to guide you in the way you should go. It's never too late to go God's way.

Share your faith and the plan God has for your life with someone. Share both the challenges and the victories you have experienced along the way. While we may have our own plans, help them understand that God's plan is always better.

𝕏 ⓘ f

@rhboydco

DDR

Devotional Readings for June 23–29, 2025

MONDAY	TUESDAY	WEDNESDAY	THURSDAY	FRIDAY	SATURDAY	SUNDAY
Purify Yourself before God	Abide in Christ, the True Vine	Seek God with All Your Heart	Christ Is among His Gathered People	Christ Is with Us Always	Joy in God's Presence	Fullness of The Lord Is in This Place
Genesis 35:1–7	John 15:1–8	Jeremiah 29:8–14	Matthew 18:15–20	Matthew 28:16–20	Psalm 16	Genesis 28:10–22

JACOB MARKS GOD'S FAITHFULNESS

BACKGROUND PASSAGE: GENESIS 28:1–22; 33:17–20; 35:1–7
PRINT PASSAGE: GENESIS 28:10–22

RESOURCES: *New National Baptist Hymnal 21st Century Edition,*
Boyd's Commentary for the Sunday School

KEY VERSE: And Jacob rose up early in the morning, and took the stone that he had put for his pillows, and set it up for a pillar, and poured oil upon the top of it. And he called the name of that place Bethel: but the name of that city was called Luz at the first. (Genesis 28:18–19, KJV)

Intro

In 2024, the Göbekli Tepe's lunisolar calendar has been deemed the oldest calendar in the world. This calendar, according to research, consists of twelve lunar months and eleven additional days, closely tracking the phases of the sun, moon, and constellations. Calendars fall into four categories—lunisolar, solar, lunar and seasonal. What we use today is called the Gregorian calendar (first introduced in 1582), which makes it easier to calculate leap year.

Today, we live in a fast–paced world, where time seems to pass quickly. A calendar can help us keep our many schedules, lists, appointments, and needs organized. Also, we can use calendars to mark when special events, such as holidays, anniversaries, and birthdays, take place. One special use of a calendar is that it helps us look back at dates, reminding us of special occasions like graduations, weddings, baptisms, the birth of a new baby, or days and moments we deem worthy of remembrance.

On one occasion, biblical patriarch Jacob needed a calendar. He experienced an unusual dream in which God appeared to him, promising that the blessings of Abraham and Isaac—his grandfather and father—would pass on to him. God passed on the blessing to make him a great nation. This was a momentous occasion. Since Jacob did not have a calendar, he used a stone to mark this occasion and to remember the graciousness of God.

Think About It

Has God created a special, spiritual moment in your life? How have you commemorated that moment and used it to impact the lives of people around you?

_____

_____

_____

_____

1. God Made Jacob a Promise (Genesis 28:10–15)

King James Version	NRSVue
AND Jacob went out from Beersheba, and went toward Haran.	JACOB left Beer-sheba and went toward Haran.
11 And he lighted upon a certain place, and tarried there all night, because the sun was set; and he took of the stones of that place, and put them for his pillows, and lay down in that place to sleep.	**11** He came to a certain place and stayed there for the night, because the sun had set. Taking one of the stones of the place, he put it under his head and lay down in that place.
12 And he dreamed, and behold a ladder set up on the earth, and the top of it reached to heaven: and behold the angels of God ascending and descending on it.	**12** And he dreamed that there was a ladder set up on the earth, the top of it reaching to heaven; and the angels of God were ascending and descending on it.
13 And, behold, the Lord stood above it, and said, I am the Lord God of Abraham thy father, and the God of Isaac: the land whereon thou liest, to thee will I give it, and to thy seed;	**13** And the Lord stood beside him and said, "I am the Lord, the God of Abraham your father and the God of Isaac; the land on which you lie I will give to you and to your offspring;
14 And thy seed shall be as the dust of the earth, and thou shalt spread abroad to the west, and to the east, and to the north, and to the south: and in thee and in thy seed shall all the families of the earth be blessed.	**14** and your offspring shall be like the dust of the earth, and you shall spread abroad to the west and to the east and to the north and to the south; and all the families of the earth shall be blessed in you and in your offspring.
15 And, behold, I am with thee, and will keep thee in all places whither thou goest, and will bring thee again into this land; for I will not leave thee, until I have done that which I have spoken to thee of.	**15** Know that I am with you and will keep you wherever you go, and will bring you back to this land; for I will not leave you until I have done what I have promised you."

Know It

The familiar story of Jacob and Esau is the story of twin brothers who are divided because of trickery. When their father, Isaac is dying, Jacob, with Rebekah's help, cheats Esau out of his father's blessing. Since Esau is a hairy man and Jacob has smooth skin, their mother places hairy fur on Jacob and sends him to his father with his favorite stew.

Isaac then unwittingly blesses Jacob, giving him the blessing that belongs to Esau, his oldest son. Isaac soon discovers what he has done, and Rebekah sends Jacob away to prevent him from falling into the clutches of his angry brother. Certainly, Esau would have killed Jacob had he not run away. After the deception, Isaac sends Jacob to Laban, Rebekah's brother, in Paddan Aram to find a wife. Jacob risks traveling alone through unfriendly Canaanite territories. Even though God had proclaimed it as the Promised Land for His people, Canaan did not yet belong to the Jews. In light of this, Jacob's travel absolutely required God's protection.

One evening during his travels, Jacob lays his head on a stone to sleep for the night. As he sleeps, he dreams that the place where he lies transforms. He sees a stairway, or ladder, reaching from earth to heaven and angels of God ascending and descending on it. It seems that this place provides access to God. Some have compared the structure in Jacob's dream to the "Tower of Babel," but while the ladder in Jacob's dream extends from heaven, the "Tower of Babel" extends from earth. As dramatic as the ladder from heaven and the angels were, the main element in the dream was God Himself who was standing at the top of the ladder.

In the dream, God extends to Jacob the covenant promise He had given to Abraham and Isaac. God tells Jacob that he is laying on the land of promise, that his descendants will live there in great number—they will be like the dust of the earth, God says. Moreover, all the people of the earth will be blessed because of Jacob and his descendants. Then, in verse 15, God makes additional promises to Jacob: God marks this moment with a promise to sustain, protect, and remain present with Jacob until all that He has spoken is accomplished.

2. Jacob Responds to His Dream (Genesis 28:16–17)

King James Version	NRSVue
16 And Jacob awaked out of his sleep, and he said, Surely the Lord is in this place; and I knew it not.	**16** Then Jacob woke from his sleep and said, "Surely the Lord is in this place—and I did not know it!"
17 And he was afraid, and said, How dreadful is this place! this is none other but the house of God, and this is the gate of heaven.	**17** And he was afraid, and said, "How awesome is this place! This is none other than the house of God, and this is the gate of heaven."

Jacob awakens from his sleep, likely startled by such a heralding dream, yet blessed by the awareness of God's presence in his space. Jacob responds to God's presence with fear, not because he is timid, but because God is great. Jacob's reaction to God's presence reflects the response that anyone who honors and respects God as Lord and Creator should have. In today's language, Jacob might have awakened and said, "Awesome!" He had a dream and experience he might never forget! We apply the word "awesome" to anything that has a great impression upon us—something that leaves us in "awe." But for Jacob, the word means God has been with him. He recognizes that the place where he lay down to sleep is special because God's presence is there. He refers to the physical space as God's house and the entryway to God's dwelling.

3. God Took Jacob as His Own (Genesis 28:18–22)

King James Version	NRSVue
18 And Jacob rose up early in the morning, and took the stone that he had put for his pillows, and set it up for a pillar, and poured oil upon the top of it.	**18** So Jacob rose early in the morning, and he took the stone that he had put under his head and set it up for a pillar and poured oil on the top of it.
19 And he called the name of that place Bethel: but the name of that city was called Luz at the first.	**19** He called that place Bethel; but the name of the city was Luz at the first.
20 And Jacob vowed a vow, saying, If God will be with me, and will keep me in this way that I go, and will give me bread to eat, and raiment to put on,	**20** Then Jacob made a vow, saying, "If God will be with me, and will keep me in this way that I go, and will give me bread to eat and clothing to wear,
21 So that I come again to my father's house in peace; then shall the Lord be my God:	**21** so that I come again to my father's house in peace, then the Lord shall be my God,
22 And this stone, which I have set for a pillar, shall be God's house: and of all that thou shalt give me I will surely give the tenth unto thee.	**22** and this stone, which I have set up for a pillar, shall be God's house; and of all that you give me I will surely give one-tenth to you."

NOTES:

When morning finally arrives, Jacob does not want the moment to be forgotten. God had visited him in a dream, so he wants to create a memorial. We would mark the day in our calendars as a reminder that God had been there. But Jacob does more. He honors God by making it a place of worship. Using the stone that he slept on, Jacob pours oil on it and consecrates it to God. Jacob uses the name he called the place the night he had the dream—Bethel—"the house of God."

Jacob then makes a vow to God, restating the promise God made to him. He, however, makes it more specific. Jacob adds to God's promise necessities like food to eat and clothes to wear. He vows that if God provides for him in these ways, so that he might come again to his father's home, God will surely be his God. Jacob seals his vow by declaring the stone as a pillar, or altar, and house of worship. To further mark how special this moment is, Jacob vows to give God a tenth of all that he receives. Jacob exhibits the faith of his ancestors, Isaac and Abraham, here. For the first time, he comes face-to-face with God, and from that moment, his life is forever changed.

Remember It

Jacob, the son of Isaac and grandson of Abraham, had to make his own way. Even though his journey was launched through deception, God honored him to be the one who would continue the blessed line of Abraham. God did not want Jacob to live on the faith of Isaac or Abraham, Jacob needed his own faith. Therefore, God appeared to Jacob through an extraordinary dream. In the dream, God gave Jacob the same covenant promise he had given his father and grandfather. Jacob and his descendants would be numerous and bless all the families of the earth. Jacob responded by creating a place of worship and making a vow to follow God. May we respond to God's grace the same way.

● ●

Hear It

Did you know you can pray the lyrics of a song? Download and read aloud the lyrics to the song, "I Have Decided to Follow Jesus." Offer the words as a prayer to reinforce your commitment to Christ.

Get Social
Start an online conversation about **#TIME**. Share your views and tag us @ rhboydco and use #rhboydco.

Live It

Jacob had a personal relationship with God. The same is true for us. Evaluate whether you are living the faith of someone else or of your own. If you are living someone else's faith, seek ways to connect to Christ personally and authentically. Begin by drawing closer to Him in prayer.

Share It

Share with someone the story of Jacob, his ancestral promises, and his face-to-face encounter with God. Encourage that we all need to encounter God the same way. That is, heritage or not, we all need to meet God for ourselves.

@rhboydco

Devotional Readings for June 30–July 6, 2025

DDR

	MONDAY	TUESDAY	WEDNESDAY	THURSDAY	FRIDAY	SATURDAY	SUNDAY
	Living in God's Presence	Anointed by the Holy One	Remember Israel's Redemption	Rejoice before the Lord	Judah Has Become God's Sanctuary	The Father and I Are One	Jesus Learns in His Father's House
						John	
	Psalm 27	1 John 2:20-28	Deuteronomy 16:1-10	Deuteronomy 16:11-17	Psalm 114	10:22-30, 34-38	Luke 2:41-52